these bold recipes for faux fancy but simple meals—*and* cocktails.

Mamrie Hart, *New York Times* best-selling author, comedian, podcast host, and longtime vegetarian, has whipped up mouthwatering meat-free meals and snacks on her socials for years. With her millions of fans and followers eating up her content and clamoring for her recipes, she delivers all that and more with this larger-than-life debut cookbook. *All I Think About Is Food* features more than 100 tantalizing dishes and spirited cocktails organized into themed-out dinner parties. With her unique spin on Southern tapas to her irreverent take on a steakhouse and an all-aphrodisiac date night, each chapter delivers on flavor and fun. They also each include a "morning-after fill," clever recipes for jazzing up your leftovers. Fabulous photography, a vivacious design, and Hart's signature warmth and humor make this book the life of the party for every campy home cook.

All I Think About Is Food

All I Think About Is Food

A VEGETARIAN COOKBOOK THAT'LL KEEP THE PARTY GOING

MAMRIE HART

Countryman Press

An Imprint of W. W. Norton & Company
Independent Publishers Since 1923

For information about permission to reproduce
selections from this book, write to Permissions,
Countryman Press, 500 Fifth Avenue, New York,
NY 10110

For information about special discounts for bulk
purchases, please contact W. W. Norton Special Sales
at specialsales@wwnorton.com or 800-233-4830

Manufacturing by RRD Asia
Book design by Evi-O.Studio | Evi O. & Katherine Zhang
Art director: Allison Chi
Production manager: Devon Zahn
Interior composition by: Carole Desnoes, Ken Hansen,
Emma Ratner

Countryman Press
www.countrymanpress.com

An imprint of W. W. Norton & Company, Inc.
500 Fifth Avenue, New York, NY 10110
www.wwnorton.com

978-1-68268-953-0

10 9 8 7 6 5 4 3 2 1

CONTENTS

Introduction

From the time I open my little peepers in the morning to the time I close them at night, all I think about is food. In the shower? Food. Typing a work email? Food. In downward dog as the yoga instructor tells us to clear our minds, I'm building that night's cheese board. You could be having a very serious conversation with me, and I'll look fully immersed. I could be nodding along and even reaching over to hold your hand in support, but, mentally, I'm deciding what soup to make tomorrow.

But being obsessed with food isn't just for when I'm hungry. It's a lifestyle.

When other people crawl into bed to read the newest sexy dragon novel, I whip out my phone and read restaurant menus. These could be for a place I'm planning to go in the future, so that I can already know what I want to order. They could be the menus of a place I've been to before, and I'm just checking in to see if they've made any updates based on the season change. Or they could be places I have no intention of going to. They're not in my city. They're not even in my state. But there I am, drooling over how good the grilled Halloumi sounds at a new spot in Eugene, Oregon. I have never visited nor do I have any plans to go to Eugene, Oregon.

Sometimes I even put down the iPhone and pick up an actual cookbook. I buy cookbooks as if I am single-handedly trying to keep the publishing business alive. I've always loved cookbooks and that's why writing this one is a dream. I remember having a kid's cookbook by the brand Klutz. Remember those? They always came with a special attachment. Like the one to learn yo-yo came with a yo-yo. The cookbook, which featured cartoon bears on the cover, came with measuring spoons. I remember finding a recipe for strawberry butter and going on a quest to ask my neighbor for a few strawberries from his garden to make that recipe for a Mother's Day breakfast-in-bed surprise. I was not messing around. I brought the *The Enchanted Broccoli Forest* with me to school one day. I couldn't believe there was a whole cookbook of all-vegetarian recipes. Everyone assumed it was a mythical tale about vegetables, not a vegetarian cookbook from 1982. If you don't know it, it's written by Mollie Katzen of Moosewood Kitchen fame. And yes, I did make a pilgrimage to her restaurant in Ithaca, New York, while I was in college. You would've thought I was visiting the Taj Mahal.

But as much as I love the written word and need to make sure everyone knows I'm literate . . . I am a total sucker for food TV.

These days, TV chefs are celebrities. Guy Fieri has his own stage at music festivals. Padma Lakshmi is bikini-clad in *Sports Illustrated* and continues to be my hall pass. You could go deep into the Amazonian rainforest of Brazil, to the Pirahã tribe of only 400 people, and one of them is going to recognize a picture of Gordon Ramsay. Chefs are culinary rockstars. But—and not to sound like a hipster in 2005 Brooklyn—I liked them before they were cool.

For example. Did you know there was a cooking show on PBS called *Two Fat Ladies*? Nowadays, I cannot imagine that title ever being green lit, but '90s British programming was wild. The show featured two besties who not only taught viewers how to cook things like partridges with cabbage or watercress mousse but also drove a motorcycle with a sidecar. Childhood-me appreciated their vibe and would regularly break out an impression that my fellow sixth-graders didn't appreciate.

Square that with the fact that I had a *Martha Stewart Living* magazine subscription before I could grow armpit hair. I was the preteen who had seen every *Iron Chef* episode. And I'm not talking about the American version. I'm talking about the dubbed Japanese version, where I had never even heard of the secret ingredients. You better believe that once *Iron Chef* came to America and started filming in New York, I went to a six-hour taping by myself, and I almost passed out when the Chairman handed me a chunk of a giant Bavarian during "Battle Pretzel."

Now, even though I love reading about food and watching food on TV, rolling up my sleeves and cooking is the place I'm most happy. I've taken cooking classes all over the world, from pasta making in Italy to a mole class in Oaxaca. I studied with a foraging legend in California and now I can spot mustard greens on the side of the road that I previously would've thought were just weeds. I've gone full hippie in the North Carolina mountains and learned which mushrooms will enhance your hike versus which will cut it short (the Destroying Angel isn't just a great metal band name—it's a terrifying mushroom).

Learning to cook began as a necessity. This was in the dark ages when you couldn't find a delicious vegetarian dish on most menus, when the closest thing I could get to an entrée in my town was a 6-inch veggie sub from Subway. That's right. I'm not only a foodie. I'm a vegetarian cutie.

GASP!

If you didn't realize this was a meat-free cookbook from the word "vegetarian" on the cover, then GOTCHA! But fear not, carnivores, this is not going to be a book that tries to convince you to come to the other side. This book is filled with guilty pleasures, not guilt trips.

A little backstory: I became a vegetarian when I was eight years old. There was no traumatic incident on the farm. I didn't have to say goodbye to a pig I helped raise. I just thought it was cool, and it stuck. Isn't that the least exciting origin story you've ever heard? Don't get me wrong! Since then, I have remained vegetarian for many reasons. I love me some animals. I also think it helps balance out my carbon footprint for driving a gas-guzzling old truck and flying so much. I love the environment, but I also love my Delta status.

Now, let's talk about going out to eat. While times have changed and you can find a few tasty veggie options on most menus, occasionally we can get shortchanged.

If I go on a date night at a classy joint, I usually have about two choices on the menu, or I have to ask the waiter so many questions or requests for substitutions and omissions that by the time the order is in, the romance is squashed. A group of friends sharing a ton of appetizers is fun—except for when they look like they're at a medieval feast and you're gnawing on the breadbasket in the corner.

And then there's the flip side. You drag your friends to a vegetarian restaurant and it ends up being elevated fast food in a weird, fluorescent-lit space with a zero percent chance of a decent cocktail! And, NO, soju is not a real cocktail to me. So, rather than finishing a night out either starving or apologizing for the lack of ambience, I take matters into my own hands. I invite people over so I can mix up bevvies and dish out deliciousness at my place!

In my truest opinion, home kitchens are the new open-concept restaurants. And after perfecting some of the recipes in this book, yours will be fully booked.

HOW THIS BOOK WORKS

In these pages, you are going to find appetizers, salads, mains, sides, the works! They are organized into dinner parties, but every recipe in here stands on its own and should be looked at à la carte. Mix it up! Pick and choose from different dinner parties! There are no rules. You better believe I've had Black-Eyed Pea Cowboy Crostinis (page 157) from The Underdogs chapter alongside a Hot and Bitter Horseradish Salad (page 33) from the Fauxncy Steak House chapter, and it was divine. I've paired a Goodbye Earl cocktail (page 93) from Southern Tapas with Figs in a Blanket (page 73) from Let's Get It On . . . the Plate. These meal pairings are simply suggestions!

But, if you *do* feel like throwing a dinner party, I've got you covered. Here you will find 10 cohesive parties from top to bottom. Dinner parties give me joy. They're where I hold court, getting to cook food for all my friends and then guilt-trip them into doing all the dishes. So when it came time to write this book, I thought, let's throw 10 dinner parties.

But you'll also need something to wash it down!

Each dinner has a few original cocktails to pair with it—a perfect thing to have ready when your guests arrive. Some are refreshing, some are dessert, and all of them will get your guests (or your party of one) feeling loosey-goosey and ready to eat.

And another thing that makes this book unique? As much as I hate to admit it, I am not a big fan of leftovers. Some people live for them, but I am so easily bored. That doesn't stop me from packing up everything and putting it in my fridge only to dread cleaning my fridge a week later and wishing I'd just trashed it. If I am eating a big meal the night before, I'm not going to crave just a heated up version the next day.*

Chances are that the morning after a dinner party, you're waking up with a Category 5 hangover and your body wants something a little more comforting. Fear not! I will show you how to transform your leftovers into exactly this. Helpfully titled Morning-After Fill, each recipe requires just a few additional ingredients and takes less than 15 minutes to prep. You've got TV to watch.

---

* Except for pizza. Pizza is always the caveat.

LET'S TALK INGREDIENTS

Since the dawn of cinema, there has been a ridiculous stereotype that women just love to shop. Can't get enough of it. Whether it's a revenge spree on Rodeo Drive in *Pretty Woman* or like when Regina George pulls up in a convertible and says, "Get in loser. We're going shopping!" in *Mean Girls*, women seem to love a dressing room montage with their friends waiting outside the curtain to give them a thumbs-up or thumbs-down. Well, here's where I tell you a little secret . . .

I can't stand shopping.

Nothing sounds less appealing than spending a whole day at the mall and trying on clothes. The only way you're going to see me have a throw-down-the-Amex shopping spree is if you take me to an amazing grocery store. The kind that has produce you've never even heard of and a cheese monger who is not only handing out samples but also has that one cheese you had on vacation and haven't found since. I want freshly roasted coffee beans, a rainbow of spices, a football field of bulk bins. Nothing gets me revved up like going in with no real plan of what I want to make for dinner but figuring out what looks good that day. That's my kind of shopping. Less pants size, and more plant size!

But sadly, not everybody has access to this holy grail of grocery stores. I know I sure didn't until I moved to New York and LA. Growing up, we would have to make a dedicated trek to the nearest Whole Foods every few months to stock our house with vegetarian frozen foods and specialty ingredients. And by nearest, I mean 45 minutes away. This would be a one-two hit with the closest movie theater. A big day for us Hart kids!

Then in high school, I worked at the tiny grocery store in my town called D&J Galaxy grocery. This place was so archaic that there were no scanners. Most transactions were cash, so, one time, a fellow employee tried to rob the place by tying the safe to his truck and dragging it through town!

Even now, when I go home to visit my mom and

want to cook her dinner, I need to think about what I can find at her local Food Lion, a grocery store that sounds a lot more exotic than it is. I kept this in mind when I created all the recipes in this book. I had www.foodlion.com pulled up on my laptop and I searched for all the ingredients on this site, because there is nothing worse than being all excited to try out some new recipes from a book, then realizing the shopping list sounds like it's for a witches' brew and there's no way you're going to find those ingredients at your store. They don't have an eye of newt at Food Lion.

So, I decided, rather than leave my fellow country folks disappointed, I would really be conscious of not putting too many ingredients in here to throw you on a wild goose chase, or leaving you trying to crack the code of a decent substitution. Can you find every single food ingredient at a local grocery store chain in Middle America? No. But there are fewer than 12 in this book that you can't. Most of them can easily be grabbed on a two-day delivery from Amazon. Thank you, Overlord Bezos!

FAKING IT

The world of fake meat these days is wild. Every year, the taste and texture gets more and more accurate. I'll cook up some veggie breakfast sausage and have a mild panic attack that I accidentally got real pork. You've got vegetarian ground beef that can fool even the most hardcore carnivores. And I would be lying if I said I haven't spit it out in fear it was the real stuff!

Back in my day (cue the grandma voice) you would go to a cookout and be lucky if someone found a freezer-burned black bean patty or a massive portabella burger. . . . Speaking of, as you flip through the recipes you'll notice I'm not a big mushroom fan, especially when it's a fungi the size of a Frisbee weighing down a bun. Progress in faux meat has been a welcome change.

I love meat imposters and cook with them often, but I know they're not for everyone.

This book is all about cooking among friends, and, it turns out, only a couple of my friends are vegetarian. That isn't to say the meat eaters aren't down to eat some veggies—it would be hard for them to object when I'm the one cooking! But I have noticed more often than not, they aren't super jazzed to get their mock meat on. Sometimes this can be because soy doesn't sit right in their belly. Or maybe it's because they think, "If I'm going to eat something that is supposed to taste like chicken, I'll just eat actual chicken."

In this book, you are going to find zero fake meat. No seitan. No soy chicken. I don't even use tempeh or tofu. There are a million recipes that use these ingredients and do it well, but it was important to me to just focus on produce. By all means, add in some veggie steak (or real steak if that's your thing!), but these recipes are specifically crafted to let you veg out.

GADGETS AND GIZMOS APLENTY

Kitchen gadgets are the closest thing I have to a hoarder tendency. I can look in a cabinet right now and find a build-your-own liquor luge kit, a dehydrator, and a cotton candy machine. But don't fret; I will not ask you to fill up your precious cabinet space with overpriced things you will use once. All my favorite tools described in this book are used multiple times, and I promise you will break them out constantly for making recipes outside of these pages.

To create the recipes from this book, you will want all the usual suspects as far as supplies go: good knives, skillets, pans, and the other essentials of any kitchen. But, seeing as though I am almost as equally excited about presentation as I am about the food itself, there are a couple of extra doodads and gadgets that I use more often in my kitchen than most. That isn't to say you can't absolutely make every recipe in this book without these items, but they will make life a little easier.

MICROPLANE

Besides the fact that the name makes me think of a miniature plane, and that's just adorable, Microplane zester/graters happen to be one of the most versatile kitchen tools. They're fantastic for mincing garlic, and make zesting citrus a breeze. But where they really shine is in tableside presentations.

A Painkiller tiki drink is fantastic with nutmeg sprinkled on top, but nutmeg finely grated on top fills the room with that sweet, spicy aroma. Anyone can put cheese on a salad. But having that cheese be freshly grated in front of you, like a salty snowfall landing on your lettuce, is a sight to behold.

FOOD PROCESSOR

Sometimes I enjoy a leisurely chop, especially when Louis Prima is playing on the record player, the Chianti is flowing, and I've got nothing but time. But when the guests are showing up in 10 minutes and I haven't even started the salsa, the food processor comes in handy. It's also a perfect shortcut for when you need things diced but aren't precious about making perfect knife cuts. When I discovered I could toss a couple celery ribs, carrots, and half an onion into a food processer, and zip it into a mirepoix in three seconds flat, it shaved off so much cooking time for a soup my

jaw dropped. And when I realized I could toss in a quartered crown of cauliflower and pulse it into fresh cauli rice in a matter of seconds, a medic had to be rushed to my home.

MASON JARS (WITH LIDS)

Little ones are perfect when making salad dressings or sauces. You just plop everything in, twist on a lid, and shake that thing like a maraca. Make a big batch and use it all week. They are also fantastic for any of the quick pickling recipes in this book, as you want to do that in a glass container. The easy alternative is to use a plastic container, but don't. We have enough microplastics in our body already—sometimes I feel like I'm half Bratz doll myself. Glass jars are also ideal for any of the cocktails that call for infusions or even an Amuse Booze drop-off (page 17).

JUICER

You can absolutely make every drink in this book with a blender and cheesecloth or mesh strainer. But if you invest in a juicer, you won't regret it. I admit that this is coming from someone who does enjoy and has been known to purchase overpriced green juices and ginger shots. The way I look at it . . . a juice and shot combo is a solid twenty bucks. Seeing as my juicer was a hundred, making just a half dozen drinks at home instead of buying them makes the juicer pay for itself. You can call this "girl math." You can call me the "Rain Man of rationalizing spending."

MELON BALLER

Technically, this gadget is only called for three times in this book, so it's a frivolous purchase. Drink garnishes are so much cuter as spheres. It's one of those things that once you use it, you will be looking for stuff to ball. You will be having a ball. I like saying balls.

TORTILLA PRESS

Besides the obvious use (there's a sweet potato tortilla recipe on page 105; get excited), this press can also be used to crush spices or garlic. Press out dough for dumplings, smash broccoli . . . the possibilities are endless. And if you don't have a tortilla press, never underestimate the capabilities of a cast-iron skillet and a little muscle.

MY MIXOLOGY PHILOSOPHY

In this book, you are going to see a lot of cocktails. Now, don't get me wrong, I love me some wine. Malcolm Gladwell famously said that to be an expert in something, you need to dedicate 10,000 hours to it. I'll see your 10K and raise you 20K, plus a lifetime of wine-stained lips in the morning.

A crisp, dry Chablis with a spicy curry is heaven. A tsunami of tannins in a Nebbiolo paired with a silky, eggplant pasta is a bonified oenophile BONER (say that five times fast). How much do I love wine? I am certified as a level three in the WSET, aka sommelier training. Lots of studying. Lots of blind tasting (poor me). And I officially have bragging rights because I can immediately spot a cabernet from Coonawarra, Australia. It's a fun party trick that is equal parts impressive and useless. Sometimes you just have to spend a lot of money and time to look like a baller when you are handed the wine list.

What I love about creating cocktails, though, is the endless amounts of variety. There are so many ways to change things up and make them your own, and an endless opportunity to surprise people with something they've never had or introduce them to a classic they've never heard of that instantly becomes their favorite.

But experimenting with cocktails is expensive as hell! I'll be looking through a revered cocktail book and come across a Prohibition-era beauty that sounds incredible—that is, until I realize it requires a couple of weird liqueurs, some random bitters that are only specific to that one drink, and before you know it, I'm dropping $150 just to make the damn thing. I've had liqueurs in my cabinet for so long that their shelf is rent stabilized.

I solemnly swear to you right here and now that that won't happen here. There are a few recipes where I suggest a cocktail that does indeed have a very specific ingredient that can't be substituted . . . and by that, I mean, maybe three in this whole book. Instead, I try to make cocktails unique and fun using produce, spices, and teas. I'd rather have you infuse a liquor or a simple syrup. You can get just as much flavor while still being a saver!

Amuse Booze

During the Covid-19 pandemic of 2020, I hated not seeing my friends. But it was also that magical moment when we all got in our little homemaker vibes and would drop things off on each other's doorsteps, sneaking in a little wave to make sure the delivery was complete. While I got homegrown cherry tomatoes and puzzles, my gifts of choice were personalized cocktails in mason jars that served four, complete with a note of instructions on how to serve. I left a jar of premixed Piña Coladas that she just needed to blend with ice on my friend Jaclyn's porch when her trip to Hawaii was canceled. When my friend Scott's album hit the charts, I made a little hibiscus-infused number that I dubbed The Hi-Note and left it on his doorstep. I felt like one of those old-school milkmen, but way more fun.

Once the quarantine ended, even though we could just meet up in person and share a drink together, I loved this tradition so much that I continued it. Imagine waking up on your birthday, and your friend has dropped off a specialty Irish coffee on your doorstep. Or you're under the weather and find a "just add water" hot toddy kit in your mailbox. Then I started thinking about how I could drop off a cocktail in advance of hosting folks as a way to set the mood and even give a little insight about what would be on the menu—something they could sip on as they prepared to come over. To whet their appetite, like when a chef brings out an amuse-bouche.

If you want to try your own Amuse Booze drop-offs before you host your friends, keep in mind that you don't need to drop off 24 ounces of martini and risk your friend passing out before they make it over. Lean more toward fruity drinks, like the mules and margaritas described in this book. You're throwing a dinner party, not a *Real Housewives* reunion, after all.

A Very Important, Must-Read Note!

We are all adults here. If you don't like an ingredient and think a different one works better for your taste buds, by all means, try a swap! Also, everyone has their own parameters. Technically, Parmesan cheese isn't vegetarian because of the rennet. Worcestershire sauce isn't vegetarian because of the anchovies. Hell, there are wines that aren't vegetarian because of their filtering process. Luckily, there are always veg and vegan versions of these ingredients, so rather than preface any ingredient in question with the word *vegetarian* or *vegan,* I'm going to leave that up to you! If you don't get down with Parmesan, grab some vegan Parmesan when the recipe calls, or try a different low-moisture cheese.

The same can be said for most of the salt and pepper in this book. This could be controversial, but I never really follow the salt and pepper directions when I read a recipe. Obviously, this changes if a dish is specifically supposed to have a decent amount of one or the other, or if it's a baking recipe and you've got one shot to get that saltiness in your dough. But these are recipes that you will taste as you go, and I want you to salt and pepper as your palate sees fit!

Personally, I tend to go lower on the salt because I inevitably add a hot sauce on the finished product, which adds its own saltiness. I am such a cracked pepper fiend (I wanted to say cracked-head but thought otherwise) that I couldn't possibly direct you on how much to add based on my preferences, or you might go full Looney Tunes and have fire coming out your ears or be sneezing for weeks. So, for this book, S&P will be to your liking unless I note otherwise or find a specific measurement crucial to the dish. And remember, you can always add it, but you can't ever take it back.

Salt and pepper is a personal preference in this book. Salt-N-Pepa is *my* personal preference on a jukebox.

FAUXNCY STEAK HOUSE

This meal might make you sign
a prenup, 'cause, baby, it's rich!

There are few things I love more than a dimly lit steak house. The leather banquettes. Sinatra wafting through the old speakers. Tuxedoed servers, who you know have worked there since Jimmy Carter was president, pouring ice-cold martinis. As the kids would say, it's my VIBE.

One of my favorites is a place called the Smoke House in Burbank, California. It sits catty-corner from Warner Brothers Studios. You might recognize the lot by its infamous water tower or where the Animaniacs would wreak havoc, but I remember it as the place I would embarrass myself in auditions. This isn't an exaggeration. Ask me to recite the Lisa "Left Eye" Lopez rap from TLC's 1994 hit "Waterfalls," and I have no problem. I can and will break out the prologue to *The Canterbury Tales* in Old English that I learned my senior year of high school with ease. But ask me to memorize a simple three-page scene and perform it for casting agents, and my brain goes blank. I go *Men in Black*-memory-scrambler blank face.

Needless to say, one might want a martini after that, 2 p.m. be damned! Luckily, it always felt like 9 p.m. in the Smoke House. It would be a sunny California day at the valet stand, but the second you entered those doors, it was nighttime, baby. It would take five minutes for my eyes to adjust, and one time I considered bringing in a headlamp, prepared to spelunk to my seat.

Once the cloak of darkness lifted, you would occasionally see someone else from the audition sitting at the bar, both happy to commiserate and let the sting of the gin take away the sting of the embarrassment. I never ate at the Smoke House. I'm sure it's great. But that's the thing about steak houses for vegetarians . . . it's always a little awkward to order.

You can never really have an entrée so much as a disjointed combo of side dishes, which I understand. It's called a steak house, not a mashed potato house (although that should exist and I would invest). But they never take your three sides and put them on one respectable plate; no, they always come on their individual dishes.

For this chapter, we are bringing the steak house home. Grab your candlelight. Your jazz. Throw on a tux if you've got one. But you might want to go up a size or two because we are about to grub out.

RECIPES

"That Butternut Be Bone Marrow" Onion Dip

Serves 4

- 1 large, or 2 to 3 small butternut squash
- 2 to 3 tablespoons olive oil
- 4 sweet onions, sliced
- 4 tablespoons unsalted butter, more butter (or white wine), if needed
- 1 garlic clove, chopped
- 1 tablespoon Worcestershire
- 1½ cups cream cheese
- 1½ cups sour cream
- 1 teaspoon celery salt
- ¼ cup chives, chopped

One day while I was doing what I always do—uploading pictures of food I make to social media for approval from strangers—I got an excited DM from my friend Melissa. There in all caps it read: "DUDE WTF! IS THAT BONE MARROW?!?!?"

Melissa has known me since we were 19. She knows I'm a vegetarian. In what world would I be eating bone marrow? But here's the thing about Melissa: She eats like a 1960s ad exec whose company is footing the bill. A bacchanal beauty. Case in point, I once saw her eat a whole lobster while taking a bubble bath.

Maybe she thought I had dropped the vegetarianism. But, come on, bone marrow?! That's like breaking your sobriety with Bacardi 151, which would actually be perfect for our dessert martini in this chapter.

I went back and looked at my post. Sure enough, the butternut squash neck that I had cut down the center looked like a roasted cow bone. It got me thinking how to go whole hog (or I guess, cow) and lean in to this look-alike.

Butternut Be Bone Marrow was born. In this version, the squash is filled with a decadent caramelized onion dip. I serve it with the traditional little scooping spoon so you can grab some dip and scoop some roasted squash, smear it on toasted bread, and top with a bright herb salad. It's sweet, smoky, and addictive.

Preheat the oven to 375°F. Trim off the stem of the squash, then cut the neck off from the base. Slice the neck in half lengthwise. We're looking for a canal, a tunnel for our dip. Honestly, just google "bone marrow appetizer." That's what we're going for! Once you've gotten all the seeds scraped out, lather every part of the squash with the olive oil and put in the oven, flesh down, for 30 minutes. Go ahead and roast the base too while you're at it. While that's going down . . .

We need to caramelize the onions. The name of this game is patience. Slice the onions about ¼ inch thick. Put your butter over medium–low heat in a sauté pan that's large enough to hold all the onions or a Dutch oven. Add your onions and you're just going to stir, slow and steady, for 20 to 25 minutes. If the butter gets too low and it feels like it might burn,

add more. Or a splash of water. Or a splash of white wine. Once they look deep and luscious, take off the heat and separate them into two equal piles.

Add half of the onions to a food processor with the garlic, Worcestershire, cream cheese, sour cream, and celery salt. Give that a whirl. Once smooth, remove from the food processor into a bowl and fold in the chives. (If you put the chives in the food processor, you're going to end up with green dip!)

At this point, the butternuts are cooked. Put the base part to the side, we'll use that tomorrow, and focus on the necks. Simply scoop the onion dip into the neck until it's flush with the sides. Then give a good chop to the other half of the caramelized onions and spread on top.

Dirty Caper

FAUXNCY STEAK HOUSE

Makes 1 cocktail

Splash of dry vermouth
**3 ounces of super dry gin (or you
  can go vodka if you prefer)**
1 ounce caper berry brine
Caper berry for garnish

I live for the fantasy of rolling up to a hot bartender, ordering a martini, then giving a wink and saying, "Make it extra dirty." The only problem is, I am not a fan of dirty martinis. I can deal with an olive. I'd even go so far as to say I enjoy them (especially thanks to the recipe for The Best Damn Olives You've Ever Had, page 71). However, the idea of just guzzling olive brine is a no-go for me. But fret not. My dirty days are still doable!

Enter the caper berry. She's salty! She's new! She's unexpected!

Which is how I hope people describe me when I enter a room.

One crucial thing before you dive in to this recipe is . . . the best-made martinis are those that start with booze that is freezing cold. Shaking a martini is part of its mystique, but half of your drink will become melted ice if you use room-temperature liquor.

Keep it in the freezer, dahlings! The alcohol level will never let it reach the point of freezing. The same could be said for me if I were accidentally locked outside during a blizzard.

I prefer my martinis dry. So what I do is pour a little bit of vermouth in a cold glass, swirl it around, and dump it out before sticking the glass in the freezer again while I make the drink. However, if you like your martini less dry, add your vermouth in during this next part.

Combine the vermouth, gin, and brine in a shaker full of ice. Get your bicep workout in, shaking for about 30 seconds, before pouring the martini into that prechilled martini glass. Garnish with a caper berry.

Artichokes Rockefeller

Serves 4

**6 cups fresh spinach or 1 cup
  frozen, defrosted and drained**
¼ cup unsalted butter
¼ cup shallot diced
½ cup onion diced
1 garlic clove minced
1 tablespoon vermouth
Pinch of nutmeg
¼ cup Parmesan
Splash of heavy cream
**One 14-ounce can baby
  artichokes, rinsed**
1½ cups all-purpose flour
½ tablespoon Old Bay Seasoning
1 egg, beaten
**2 to 3 cups vegetable oil or
  peanut oil**
Salt
Lemon wedges for serving

One of my favorite steak house side dishes is creamed spinach, but there's a threshold with it. After a few spoonfuls, I'm sitting pretty. After spoonful 10, I feel like I'm eating bougie baby food. Or like you brought Granny to the steak house, and she forgot to put her teeth in. Don't get me wrong, it's delicious, but completely devoid of texture.

Enter Artichokes Rockefeller! Just like the oyster version, we are whole frying a crispy bite to put on top of our spinach . . . but instead of an oyster, it's a crunchy golden baby artichoke.

First, let's get the spinach made. Melt the butter over medium heat before adding in the shallots, garlic, and onions. Sauté for 3 to 4 minutes.

Once they are are sweated, add the vermouth, spinach, and nutmeg. If you are using fresh spinach and are worried there's too much, remember that spinach is the opposite of a "grower not a show-er." It's going to shrink quicker than George Costanza in a cold pool. Once it's wilted, probably after 2 minutes, stir in the Parmesan and your splash of heavy cream. Set that over low heat as we crisp up the artichokes.

Time for the dredge station! Mix the flour and half of the Old Bay in one small bowl. Then the beaten egg and remaining half of Old Bay in another. One by one, coat your artichokes in flour, then egg mixture, before one more coating in the flour.

Heat enough oil to be able to deep-fry. Ideally, the oil should be about 370°F, but if you don't have a thermometer, just make sure it's hot enough by dropping in a few bread crumbs and see if they crisp up. Once the oil is hot, carefully drop in your artichokes until crispy brown. Pull them from the oil, set on a paper towel to drain, and hit them with salt.

Arrange your artichokes on top of the spinach and serve with lemon wedges and tiny, adorable forks.

Waldorf Fizz

Makes 1 cocktail

For the Green Juice
YIELDS 6 CUPS

Apples (see steps for quantities)
Green grapes
Celery

For the Cocktail
1 egg white
2 ounces white rum
2 ounces Green Juice
1 ounce simple syrup
2 dashes walnut bitters
 (see Sidenote)
Garnishes of choice

If you want to skip eating the salad course and drink it instead . . . now's your chance!

This cocktail takes the iconic Waldorf salad, invented over 100 years ago at the Waldorf Astoria hotel in NYC, and deconstructs it. I know what you're thinking. Mamrie, calling something "deconstructed" is for when a *Chopped* contestant doesn't plate their dish in time, and they need that word as a cop-out to rationalize how bad it looks.

That is not the case here. Flexing your bar skills, this cocktail uses (almost) all the ingredients of this super old-school starter and turns it into a surprising sip. And before you google what goes in a Waldorf salad and start to freak out that we are putting mayonnaise in a drink, how dare you! I would never! But we are going to use a vital ingredient of mayo, an egg, particularly the egg white, to give this drink a creamy top, which will act as a buoy for some garnishes. I do a little mix of crushed walnuts tossed in sugar and a few celery slivers.

In a cold press juicer, make your green juice. Just make sure it's equal parts apple, grape, and celery. This is my method, seeing as some apples are juicier than others and we want equal parts, I will juice everything into one container. Once you've juiced enough apples to make 2 cups, move on to the grapes, and then the celery. If you don't have a juicer, put them in a blender and go to town. Then run your pulpy juice through a cheesecloth or super-fine mesh strainer to get out all the delicious debris. You can save this green juice as a healthy pick-me-up for the next morning, or freeze for future use.

In an empty shaker, add the egg white, rum, 2 ounces of the green juice, and bitters and give them a shake for a solid minute, which will feel weird as there's no ice to make noise. This is called a dry shake. Then add ice and re-shake for another 30 seconds to get it cold before pouring your drink through a mesh strainer into your serving glass (I recommend a coupe glass!). What you should be left with is a bright green drink topped with a thick, creamy layer. Use that egg white layer like a shelf for all your garnishes.

Sidenote
If you don't feel like buying walnut bitters, fear not! This drink will still be delicious without them. The bitters just give it a little "je ne sais quoi," which is French for "What the fuck is this?"

Hot and Bitter Horseradish Salad

Serves 4

For the Dressing

¼ cup balsamic vinegar
1 tablespoon honey,
   more if needed
1 tablespoon Dijon mustard
1 tablespoon grated horseradish
   (jarred), more if needed
Pinch red pepper flakes (optional)
Juice of half a lemon
1 garlic clove, minced
¼ cup olive oil
Salt
Pepper

For the Salad

1 cup basil
2 cups chopped romaine
2 cups chopped small radicchio
2 cups arugula
1 cup shredded carrot
1 cup diced cucumbers
1 cup cooked chickpeas

Half of the reason for creating this salad is to just let people look at the menu and say, "Hot and bitter? Is this thing named after my ex?!" This is no ordinary chopped salad, which, while delicious, can get boring. This salad is unexpected . . . like when my ex served me divorce papers. (That's the last ex joke, I swear.)

Grab whatever veggies and herbs your body is craving, but make sure there's an element of bitterness to play off the sweet-and-heat dressing. Here's how I make mine.

To make the dressing: In a bowl, combine all the dressing ingredients but the oil, salt, and pepper and whisk. Then slowly pour in your oil with one hand while whisking with the other so that it emulsifies. This makes it less likely to separate. Add salt and pepper as you please. Does it have enough of a kick? If not, add more horseradish or even a pinch of red pepper flakes. Is it too spicy for you? Add a little more honey.

Now to make the salad. If you are adding basil to your salad, let's get all fancy-like and do a chiffonade. Simply stack the basil leaves on top of each other and roll them together. Once you've got your basil tube (or joint) take a sharp knife and slice across into thin strips. You're left with little ribbons of basil. Ooh la la!

Toss all the salad ingredients in the dressing and you're good to go.

Smoky Tomato Grits

Serves 4

4 tablespoons butter
1 pint cherry tomatoes
1 tablespoon tomato paste
2 cups veggie broth,
  more if needed
2 cups milk (nut, cow, whichever
  you like)
1 cup uncooked grits
1 cup shredded smoked Gouda
Salt
Pepper

With any meal that has a bevy of sauces, we need something to sop it up. Sure, steak houses are known for mashed potatoes, but how many more mashed potato recipes does one need? Instead, I'm getting back to my roots and making a big pot of grits.

Some of you might say you've never had grits. And to that I say, have you had polenta? Honey, you've had grits. They are essentially the same thing except grits are usually milled once, so their texture is, dare I say, grittier? Polenta is milled multiple times for a smoother texture.

I love grits, and I am no snob about them. Give me a tiny white plastic bowl of grits at Waffle House and I am a happy lady. Of course, there I would just add butter, salt and pepper, and a little shredded cheddar. But here, we are classy. We are cooking these grits with melted tomatoes and adding grated Gouda for a smoky touch.

In a medium saucepot, add 2 tablespoons of the butter over medium–low heat before adding the tomatoes and paste. Allow to cook and burst without burning, stirring occasionally for 4 to 5 minutes. Once they look melted down, I like to take a masher and make sure they are broken up into bits.

Add the vegetable broth and milk and bring to a boil before stirring in the grits. I use fast-cooking grits, which takes only 5 to 10 minutes. But stone-ground can take up to 30, so be sure to check when you are buying your grits and cook according to the package. If you do go for slower-cooking grits, have extra veggie broth on hand in case it reduces and you need to add more before the grits are tender.

Once the grits are cooked, fold in your cheese and add salt and pepper to taste.

GRITS is also an acronym for "Girls Raised in the South" as noted by many a Cracker Barrel gift shop sweatshirt.

Asparagus Mimosa

Serves 4

1 pound asparagus
¾ cup olive oil
1 teaspoon garlic powder
½ cup capers
½ tablespoon Dijon mustard
1 tablespoon red wine vinegar
1 half lemon, juiced
1 cup chopped flat-leaf parsley
3 hard-boiled eggs, chopped (I use
  the Pickled Pink Eggs; page 90)

The first time I saw this dish on a menu I thought, *They've gone too far.* I am all about incorporating fresh juice into a cocktail, as you can see with the Waldorf Fizz (page 30), but this is madness. Well, faithful readers, I'm an idiot. It turns out that *mimosa*, when talking about French cooking, doesn't mean champagne and orange juice, but instead it means "hard-boiled eggs." I was relieved and ready to try!

First, let's blanch the asparagus by putting them in a medium saucepan of boiling water for 3 to 4 minutes before submerging in an ice bath to stop the cooking. You can make this recipe with roasting or steaming methods, or even grilling them, too. It's all a preference. Then I wipe out that saucepan to reuse for the eggs and vinaigrette.

Add the olive oil to the pan over medium heat and add the garlic powder. Garlic powder has a smaller window than fresh garlic before it burns, so toast for only 45 seconds or so before adding the capers, Dijon, red wine vinegar, and lemon juice. Let that simmer for 2 to 3 minutes.

Remove the pan from the heat and mix in your chopped egg and parsley. Plate the asparagus, then pour the chunky mimosa sauce over the top. Serve with tongs. Singing Sisqó's hit but with the words changed to the "Tong Song" is optional but encouraged.

Cauliflower Steaks with Peppercorn Bordelaise

Serves 4

For the Peppercorn Bordelaise

2 tablespoons green peppercorns (or black peppercorns for more heat)
2 cups red wine
¼ cup minced shallots
1 bay leaf
1 cup veggie stock
1 teaspoon not-beef bouillon
1 tablespoon butter

For the Cauliflower

Four ½-inch-thick cauliflower steaks
Olive oil
Salt
Pepper
1 teaspoon garlic powder
1 teaspoon paprika

Cauliflower steaks have suffered from overexposure in the past few years, but I still love them. There's something about being able to cut into your veg entrée with a fork and steak knife that makes you feel like you are sitting at the grown-up's table. Especially when it is sitting atop a sauce made of red wine and peppercorns. I serve with a rough chimichurri to add some brightness and really raise the stakes! Umm . . . steaks.

First things first; let's get the sauce started. Crush the green peppercorns with the flat side of a knife. Then add the now-crushed peppercorns,, the red wine, shallots, bay leaf, veggie stock, and bouillon to a small pot over medium–low heat with no lid. You want it at the lowest possible flame on a low steady bubble to reduce, probably 30-plus minutes. While that's doing its thing . . .

Cauliflower steaks are straightforward. Slather in olive oil, salt, and pepper and grill, right? Well, I add one step. Like most things, I like my steaks thick. Filet-style, baby. But if you throw them raw on the grill, I don't think they get cooked long enough. So, before you add anything, put your unoiled, unseasoned steaks in a 350°F oven for 10 to 12 minutes. Take them out, rub with the olive oil, salt and pepper, garlic powder, and paprika, and throw them on a hot grill just to get the char. Plate over the bordelaise and tuck into it like it's the priciest cut on the menu!

This is a bordelaise sauce but our version is "borderline lazy." It's easy as heck but nonetheless impressive.

Cherries Jubilee Daiquiri

Makes 1 cocktail

For the Daiquiri

¼ cup tart cherry juice
   (see Sidenote)
2 ounces cognac, bourbon, or
   brandy to preference
2 ounces simple syrup (brown
   sugar if possible)
6 or so frozen, pitted cherries
1 ounce lemon juice
Ice

For the Flame

Bite of cookie or pinch of bread
   or cake
¼ teaspoon lemon extract
Cinnamon

I have always loved the idea of cherries jubilee. It just sounds cute, right? Like an all-girl country group from the '60s. Or a backwoods line dancing place run by a sassy broad named Cherry with pink hair. Come on down and cut a rug at . . . Cherry's Jubilee! But more than the name, I love the presentation.

Nothing gets me more excited than a tableside presentation where there's a chance your eyebrows will be singed off. Here, we are going to skip dessert and turn the flaming classic into a frozen cocktail. Ready the fire extinguisher. Bonus: Cherry juice produces tryptophan and melatonin in the body, making it the perfect nightcap before catching some zzz's.

Add all your ingredients to a blender and pulse until smooth. If it's too slushy and you want it more solid, just add more ice until you have the consistency you want.

The fire is totally not necessary to the taste of this drink but, hot damn, if it ain't a cool presentation. When you think of a flaming drink, your brain might go to those famous Bacardi 151 drinks you drank in college. I am here to tell you there's a better way. Not only can all the 151 burn off so you're not getting the booze anyway, but, also, the fire doesn't look as cool. The 151 is so strong that all you get is a dinky little blue flame because it's burning so hot. Instead, a trick of the tiki trade is lemon extract! You could create a divot in the top of your cherry to hold some lemon extract. For this cocktail in the photo, I slid in a little cookie in the back with a few lemon extract drops on it, lit it up, and dusted it with cinnamon. Not only is the cinnamon a complementary flavor addition to the drink, but it makes the flames spark and it smells AMAZING!

Sidenote

If you want your jubilee looking like the party pictured here, the first step is to freeze your cherry juice into cubes. A ¼ cup will shake out to be 2 or 3 cubes, so if you are making lots of these, go ahead and freeze a tray or two. One less thing to help melt your drink, so consider this a "frosted tip"!

Morning-After Fill: Ooey-Gooey French Onion Grilled Cheese with Butternut Bisque

FAUXNCY STEAK HOUSE

Serves 2

Leftover List

½ cup "That Butternut Be Bone
 Marrow" Onion Dip (page 24)
Base of Roasted Squash from
 "That Butternut Be Bone
 Marrow" Onion Dip (page 24)
½ cup grated smoked Gouda from
 Smoky Tomato Grits (page 36)

New Stuff

4 slices of bread
1 tablespoon butter
2 cups veggie stock,
 more if needed
One 13.5-ounce can coconut milk
½ tablespoon garlic powder
Salt
Pepper
Pinch of nutmeg

Picture this. You had a rollicking steak house party. The guests couldn't get enough of your cocktails. The Dirty Capers were flowing and you managed to not have the fire department called from all the Jubilee Daquiris. The only thing that hurts more than realizing you didn't stack the dishwasher before going to sleep is your headache. You need comfort food and you need it fast.

Luckily, this edible hug can be whipped up in 10 minutes.

Assemble your grilled cheese by smearing onion dip on the inside of both pieces of bread before adding the Gouda. Grill it up on both sides in a large hot skillet with lots of melted butter for 2 minutes or until golden brown. It's a grilled cheese sandwich; you got this.

While that gets golden brown, take your leftover butternut squash, peel off the skin, and throw in a blender. Add the veggie stock, coconut milk, garlic powder, nutmeg, and salt and pepper to the blender with the squash. Blend until smooth, and then pour into a pot over medium heat for 5 minutes to let the flavors get to know each other. I like my soup thick, almost bisque-like, on a morning like this. If you want it thinner, simply add some more stock, but I prefer it to have some body as there's less chance of spilling it with my shaky hands. Give it a dash of nutmeg at the end if you're feeling wild!

Extra Tip

The bisque is very decadent, so I like to brighten it with a little rough chimichurri, as I do with the Cauliflower Steak (page 38). Have basil from the Hot and Bitter Horseradish Salad (page 33)? Blend a handful with olive oil for an herbaceous basil oil to dot on top.

ROOTIN' FRUITIN' SUMMER COOKOUT

A light, bright feast that makes sure you get to chill and not just stand over the grill.

othing like a good ol' sweaty, summer cookout. I love them. But what I don't love is when you show up and everything to eat is SO HEAVY.

Deviled eggs, pasta salad, potato salad, all the salads with all the mayonnaise just baking in the heat. Besides being a weekend of food poisoning waiting to happen, the last thing I want to do after eating all that dense food is to squeeze into a bathing suit and hoist my ass up into an aboveground pool.

I want my cookouts light! Refreshing! So for this one, we are making a summer menu that features fruit. But not all the go-to fruits one might think. There are lots of fruits that people assume are veggies and they just go with it. I remember the first time I found out a tomato was actually a fruit, and my tiny brain exploded! Nothing was real. This cruel world was built on lies. . . . Some might have referred to me as a dramatic child. I digress!

Along with the recipes in this chapter having a lot of fruit to boot, they also have short prep times. All the sauces, dressings, and so forth can be made well in advance, meaning you'll have only a couple things to cook on the day. After all, you should be doing cannonballs and "accidentally" losing your bikini top on impact, not babysitting the grill.

RECIPES

Watermelon Wheels

Serves 1

One ½-inch-thick watermelon
   wheel (cut as pictured)
Thinly sliced tomatoes (green are
   great if you can get)
Feta
Pickled Onions (page 228)
Mint leaves
Aged balsamic glaze
Olive oil
Optional: Sherry Shallot
   Vinaigrette (page 177), if it needs
   a little more moisture and punch

Few things are more refreshing than a summertime watermelon salad. And few things are more infuriating than seeing a person pick out all the watermelon and feta and then leave you the tomato scraps. No more!

We are putting a wedge spin on the Greek classic by cutting a whole watermelon into a wheel. That wheel serves as our base, almost like its own fruit plate. All the yummy accoutrements are then stacked on top. It's not only a showstopper but also a way to stop the watermelon thieves. Note that in the ingredient list to the left I do not put the quantities of the garnishes. That's because that wheel is like a salad version of a personal-pan pizza. Top it how you like!

Cut your watermelon all the way through so you've got yourself a pink plate of fruit. I essentially use the watermelon as my canvas, then build it up. I put down the tomatoes, since they are the biggest, then dot the whole thing with the feta. Sprinkle on the pickled onions and mint, then it's time to dress. I like giving it a big dot of balsamic on the edge so you can dip your bites into it, but this is your masterpiece to decorate how you want. A few good drizzles of a nice olive oil and grab a fork and knife.

Normal salads leave you bored? Try this gourd!

I'm All Ears Pasta Salad

Serves 4

1 pound orecchiette
¼ cup olive oil, more for the corn
¼ cup red wine vinegar
2 ears of fresh corn
2 cups Salsa Verde (page 136)
1½ cups cotija cheese,
  more for garnish
1 cup corn nuts
1 cup sliced radishes for garnish
Cilantro for garnish

Did you know that the pasta shape *orecchiette* translates to "little ears"? It's cute in theory, but kind of weird when you are chomping down on a forkful of little ears. Let's block that out for now, shall we? This salad doesn't just use ear pasta, but also ears of corn. It's got all the trappings of sweet summer corn salad with a little zippy kick from the tomatillo and crunch from the corn nuts. No boring pasta salads here!

Cook and drain the pasta, then immediately toss in your olive oil and red wine vinegar. This will help it from clumping up.

Lather the corn with olive oil and put on a hot grill, turning every few minutes until it has a slight char all over, usually 2 minutes each on all four sides. Let cool, then slice the corn kernels off the cob. Our former braces-wearers know to do this in a bowl!

Mix salsa verde with the cooked pasta, grilled corn kernels, cotija, and corn nuts. Garnish with radishes, extra cotija, and cilantro leaves.

This pasta salad is the only thing cornier than your uncle's jokes at this cookout.

BYO'Baba Ghanoush

Serves 4

1 large eggplant
Olive oil
1 teaspoon cumin
1 teaspoon paprika
1 tablespoon sumac
½ cup chopped flat-leaf parsley,
  more for garnish
4 tablespoons Tahini Sauce
  (page 229)

For Serving
Pomegranate seeds
Hazelnut Salsa Macha (page 228)
Pine nuts

Be careful, y'all. Baba ghanoush is a gateway dish for starting to like eggplant. Which is a fruit, by the way! The first time I dipped into some baba, I went in assuming it was a bowl of hummus. I was blown away. What was this earthy concoction? It was smoky. It was creamy. It was my new favorite dip. Before that, I thought eggplant was just an overrated sponge.

Whenever I make my own, though, I hate throwing away the beautiful, charred skin just to puree everything. This open-faced take is faster and better looking. Serve with crackers, lavash, or crusty bread.

Coat the eggplant in a healthy dose of olive oil and give it a few pokes of a fork so it doesn't explode before putting it on the grill. Once on the grill, turn it every couple of minutes until it is blackened and tender to the touch of your tongs. If it's charring up too fast but not done, move to the higher rack off the heat, or grab a cast iron, and let it continue to roast in the closed grill like an oven for 10 minutes or until fully tender. Take it off the heat to let it cool down till you are able to handle it.

Cut a slit down the center of the eggplant and open it up like you're performing open heart surgery. Dump in your cumin, paprika, sumac, parsley, and half your tahini sauce. Then take two forks to mix in and almost shred the inside like you would chicken or pulled pork. What you're trying to do is make the inside creamy and dip-like without breaking the outside skin. When it's a good consistency, drizzle the rest of your tahini sauce, dust with sumac if you have it, and garnish with more parsley and whatever else sounds good!

Pearl and Pesto Stuffed Peaches

Serves 4

4 peaches
Olive oil
3 cups cooked pearl couscous
1 cup Pistachio Pesto (page 228)
1 cup diced cucumber
1 cup diced snap peas
Basil leaves for garnish

I had an unhealthy obsession with the book *James and the Giant Peach* when I was little. I was so jealous of this kid who got to live inside a sweet fruit and make besties with all these big-ass bugs. Looking back, it is an incredibly messed up book and child protective services would have been called on those aunts. What was Roald Dahl smoking?

That I don't know, but I do know smoking up a grill and getting a little char on some juicy peaches is one of summer's greatest treats. Grilling the peaches allows the sugar in the fruit to caramelize, which is a perfect contrast to the garlicky pesto.

Halve your peaches, removing the pits. I had to watch a YouTube tutorial the first time and it's basically like halving an avocado but more awkward. Once you have conquered it, rub your halves with olive oil and put on a medium-hot grill for 2 to 3 minutes on each side.

Once you've got good char marks, take off the heat and let them cool. Take a melon baller and scoop out about half of the peach's flesh, leaving you with a mini peach bowl. Save this cooked peach flesh for your Peachy Keen Spicy Mezcalrita (page 55).

Mix your couscous with the pesto, bell pepper, cucumber, and snap peas, then load into your hollow peaches. Garnish with basil leaves.

Peachy Keen Spicy Mezcalrita

Makes 1 cocktail

For the Peach Puree
1 cup grilled peach meat
1 tablespoon lemon juice
1 teaspoon sugar
Water, if necessary

For the Cocktail
1 ounce peach puree
2 slices of Fresno or jalapeño chili
2 ounces mezcal
1½ ounces lime juice
½ ounce agave
Salt or Tajín for your rim (optional)

You didn't think we were going to waste that grilled peach meat from the Pearl and Pesto Stuffed Peaches recipe (page 52), did you? Not in this house/patio area. This drink, which can be served up, on the rocks, or frozen, is a perfect punch of sweet summer flavor with smoky mezcal—like the good girl dating the bad boy.

If you think you'll be serving a ton of these, simply grill up extra peach halves like in the previous recipe and then double or triple the puree recipe. This puree is fantastic to make while peach season is poppin' and then store in an airtight container in the freezer. Then, at your next brunch, simply plop a small scoop of frozen goodness into your prosecco and watch as it melts and transforms your bubbles into a Bellini. And if it's not peach season, skip the grilling and just make it with thawed, frozen peaches.

For the peach puree, combine the peach meat, lemon juice, and sugar in a blender and blend until smooth. The peach should be juicy from the grilling, but you can always add a splash of water if necessary. Strain through a sieve.

In a shaker full of ice, add a couple of slices of Fresno or jalapeño chili. Muddle like mad, then add the peach puree, mezcal, and lime juice. Shake it good and cold, then pour into your glass of choice. Bonus points if it's rimmed with salt, or Tajín but it's a pool party and I really don't need any extra bloating.

A couple of these will have you feeling just peachy.

Okra Skewers with Kickin' Remoulade

Serves 4

For the Skewers

1 pound okra (I like the smaller ones better)
Olive oil
Creole seasoning
Sea salt
1 lemon

Kickin' Remoulade

½ cup stone-ground mustard
½ cup sour cream or mayo
2 tablespoons apple cider vinegar
2 tablespoons horseradish
1 tablespoon honey
1 garlic clove
¼ cup diced pickle
Juice of half a lemon
Couple dashes of your favorite hot sauce

Okra is a very divisive ingredient. Some people refuse to eat plain okra because of its texture (plus okra pods are often called lady's fingers, an unfortunate nickname). Naturally, the go-to solution is chopping the okra pods up and frying them so hardcore that people don't even know what they are eating. But I have a different favorite way to make this controversial fruit acceptable to all (or most): grilling them on high heat. In my experience, it zaps any gooeyness right out of there. Dunk them in a remoulade that is amped up with horseradish for a little spice, and they're delicious!

Skewer up your whole okras, then rub with olive oil and cover with creole seasoning. If you're using Old Bay Seasoning, be conscious of the salt that's already mixed in. Don't overdo it. I like a lot of seasoning, but I don't want it to be a sodium bomb, so I will use a no-salt-added blend and then hit my okras with sea salt once they're off the grill.

Put them on the hot grill, about 4 minutes on each side. Also, halve your lemon and give the cut sides a char while the skewers cook. Once you take off the skewers, hit them with a little salt and squeeze of the lemon juice right before serving.

Meanwhile, stick all the remoulade ingredients except the pickle in a food processor and blend until creamy. I like to stir in my dill pickle last so as not to bruise it.

Pull-and-Peel Spring Onions with Romesco

Serves 4

3 red bell peppers
¼ cup plus 2 tablespoons
   extra-virgin olive oil
2 garlic cloves
2 tablespoons red wine vinegar
1 teaspoon smoked paprika
1 teaspoon lemon zest
2 tablespoons lemon juice
¼ teaspoon cayenne pepper
½ cup toasted almonds
1 pound spring onions
Salt
Pepper

This dish is my ode to an episode of Anthony Bourdain's *No Reservations* that has haunted me for years. In it, he goes to Spain during their annual calçot season. Calçots are big green onions from Catalunya. But these particular onions have a location designation, meaning that to earn its namesake they have to be grown in that certain region. Like the champagne of scallions. Every year, in the bitter cold of January, the sleepy town of Valls has a massive festival where these onions are charred over open flames and served alongside bowls of nutty romesco and zero utensils. Long tables are filled with people getting their hands dirty while peeling back layer upon layer of the onion and dunking them into a vibrant sauce. All paired with tons of Spanish red wine.

Bourdain loved it. I'd love it. But I just haven't been able to bring myself to spend money to fly to Spain in the dead of winter. Every time my hand hovers on the "purchase flight" button while rewatching that episode for the tenth time, I chicken out, knowing that Europe in the summer is much more my vibe. Bummed to forever have this culinary holy grail pass me for another year, until . . . duh, Mamrie. Make it yourself. It doesn't have to be a regionally dedicated spring onion. You've got onions at the grocery store. And it doesn't have to be in the dead of winter. Break these things out at a BBQ!

First, let's make the romesco since it takes time for the peppers to cool. You are more than welcome to make your romesco with jarred roasted red bell peppers. There is no shame. I've done this several times myself. But because we are firing up the grill anyway, rub your peppers with one of the tablespoons of olive oil and toss on a medium-high heat grill, turning once they char and feel soft and are blackened all around. It depends how hot your grill is, but this should take 3 to 4 minutes on each of the four sides.

Once they are blistered up and black on all sides, take them off the heat, toss them in a bowl, and cover with a dish towel or plastic wrap. Let those bad boys steam for 5 to 10 minutes. Once they are cooled, simply peel away the charred skin, then the seeds, membrane, and stems.

Throw your peeled red peppers in a food processor with the rest of the romesco ingredients: the garlic cloves (which you can leave whole as they are about to be pulverized), red wine vinegar, paprika, lemon zest and juice, cayenne pepper, roasted almonds, and ¼ cup of olive oil. What we want is for it to be somewhat smooth with a toothsome texture from the almonds.

For the onions, simply do what you did with the peppers. Take that last tablespoon of olive oil and coat your onion from bulb to top. Give them some salt and pepper, then toss on the hot grill. The outer layers will char up. Cook time depends on their thickness. If you are cooking big spring bulbs, you can cook for 6 to 8 minutes, turning frequently. If you do this with scallions, 2 to 3 minutes total is plenty. Once there is a slight char on the stems, take them off the heat. Let cool for a moment before diving in with your hands. Peel back each layer almost like you're husking corn, except these layers become more and more tender the further in you get. Dip straight into the romesco and put it down the hatch like a Catalonian.

Reprimand any heathen for double-dipping by throwing them in the pool.

Banana Daiquiri with Magic Shell

Makes 1 cocktail

For the Cocktail
½ **frozen banana**
2 **ounces rum**
2 **ounces vanilla-flavored milk (oat, nut, whatever your preference)**
1 **ounce banana liqueur**
Ice

For the Magic Shell
½ **cup of your favorite chocolate**
1 **tablespoon solid coconut oil**

The key to a good banana daiquiri is all in the banana liqueur. Yes, this is one of those few moments that I will urge you to invest in a good bottle. We've all had the cheap, neon yellow–labeled liquor in college that would leave you waking up with 99 problems. Nowadays, they make some high-quality stuff that tastes like a real banana and not just like licking a banana scratch-and-sniff sticker. I like using a high-quality dark, aged rum to make it more a-PEEL-ing. But Bacardi works just as well. Your friends are already playing naked Marco Polo in the pool, I doubt they are rum snobs.

But, this isn't just the best dang banana daiquiri you've ever had—we are also paying homage to the frozen chocolate-dipped bananas they serve up everywhere from Disneyland to *Arrested Development*. Bonus: You don't have to walk around with an incredibly phallic-looking snack on a stick . . . unless you're into that sort of thing.

Blend all the daiquiri ingredients in a blender, adding ice as you see fit to get to the consistency you want. When it's done, I like to pile it high in a glass and chuck it into the freezer as I get the magic shell together. The colder the daiquiri is, the less chance of the magic shell melting and, instead, instantly hardening.

For the magic shell, simply melt the chocolate and coconut oil together. This can be in an old-school double broiler or doing small bursts of 20-second intervals in the microwave with stirs in between. Once it's a chocolate-sundae-syrup consistency, pour over your daiquiri. Watch it harden and grab a spoon to crack it!

This drink is literally bananas.

Morning-After Fill:
Shock the System Shakshuka

Serves 2

Leftovers

2 cups mix of chopped Okra Skewers (page 56), Pull-and-Peel Spring Onions (page 58), Pearl and Pesto Stuffed Peaches (page 52), eggplant from the BYO'Baba Ghanoush (page 51), and corn from I'm All Ears Pasta Salad (page 48)

½ cup romesco sauce (from the Pull-and-Peel Spring Onion recipe (page 58)

Pesto from the Pearl and Pesto Stuffed Peaches (page 52) for garnish

Cotija from the I'm All Ears Pasta Salad (page 48) for garnish

New Stuff

Olive oil
1 garlic glove, minced
1 tablespoon cumin
1 tablespoon paprika
One 28-ounce can crushed tomatoes
4 eggs
Choice of herbs for garnish
Crusty bread

Let's face it. You went a little hard on the Banana Daquiris (page 61) and passed out with chlorine in your hair. That's OK. No judgment here. We're going to fix you right up while cleaning out your fridge. If you've never had shakshuka, it's perfect for a morning after. You get your spice, your runny egg, and your pop of cheese. And scooping it up with crusty bread will absolutely demolish your hangover.

Chop up 2 cups worth of any leftover okra, spring onions, and eggplant. If you've got leftover stuffed peaches, take out the couscous and eat it cold before chopping up the peach. If you've got extra grilled corn, let it join the party. Warm up a little oil in a large sauté pan over medium heat, add your garlic, cumin, and paprika and stir for 1 minute before chucking in your leftovers. Sauté for 2 to 3 minutes.

Dump in the can of tomatoes and the leftover romesco. Give everything a big stir. Once that goodness is bubbling, take your spoon and create divots in your sauce mixture, almost like a little cubby for your eggs. Crack the eggs into their little beds, cover the pan, and let the eggs steam. I let them go until the egg yolks are over-medium, then take off the heat for about 5 minutes, but you can always let them go longer if you aren't a fan of runny yolks.

Dot with leftover pesto, cotija, or any herbs and serve with crusty bread. So friggin' good.

This breakfast will have you all shook up.

LET'S GET IT ON ... THE PLATE

Tasty nibbles that'll have you loosening your pants—before you want to rip them off.

With this meal, we are diving in to the world of aphrodisiacs. Aphrodisiacs have always fascinated me. When I first learned about them, I was too young to grasp their subtle effects and thought, "Oh god! I can't be all horned up at Thanksgiving! What will grandma think?!" I thought they acted like Viagra or those Rhino 69 pills they keep behind the counter at the gas station. I was wrong.

Aphrodisiacs are foods that have libido-increasing qualities. This could be as blatant as encouraging extra blood flow to certain regions.

This meal goes hard (wink wink) in the aphrodisiac department from top to bottom. But before we dive in, please know that I am in no way fiscally responsible for any effects that might take place nine months after this meal. However, might I suggest "Mamrie" as a possible name . . . .

At this meal, no utensils are required. We're about to get handsy.

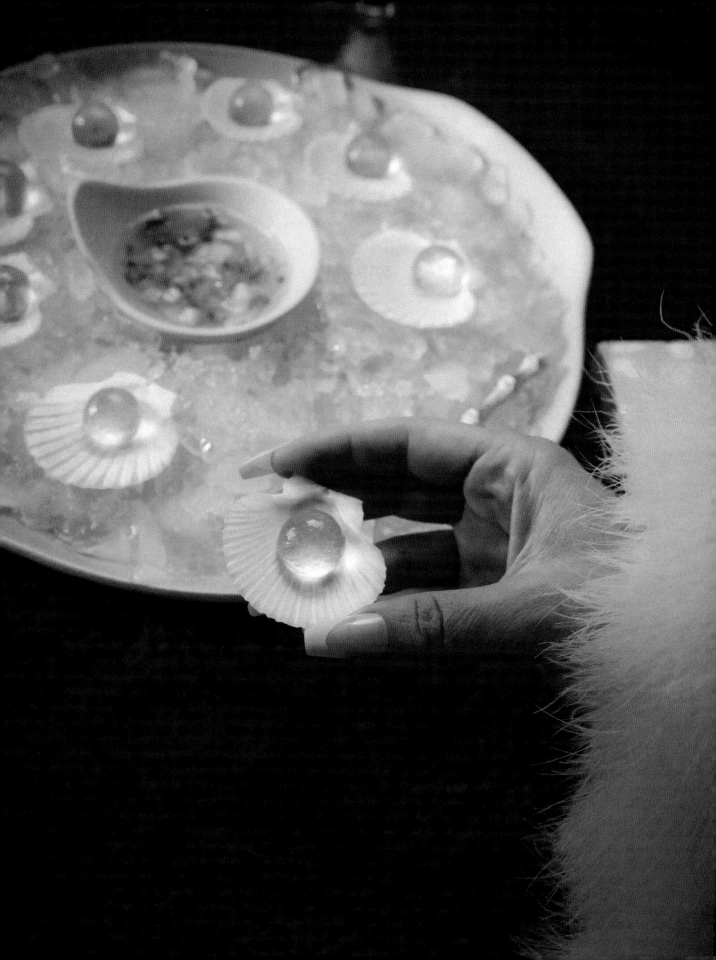

Lychee Little Necks with Strawberry Mignonette

Serves 4

For the Little Necks
1 cup citrus (or plain) vodka
1 cup juice from canned lychees
1½ teaspoons clear agar-agar

For the Strawberry Mignonette
**¼ cup combo of minced
  strawberries and lychees**
¼ cup champagne
1 tablespoon lemon juice
**Splash of very cold citrus vodka
  (optional)**

Lychees are chock-full of potassium, copper, and vitamin C, which are libido enhancers. You know what else increases my libido? Jell-O shots. But gone are the days of wanting to down a fruit punch Jell-O shot from a disintegrating Dixie cup, like I would in college. I wanted to find a way to make them romantic. Enter Jell-O shots made to look like a seafood tower. Makes sense, right?

Oysters and clams are known aphrodisiacs. Yes, they have the science to back it up but, part of me thinks it's because of how you eat them. The act of watching your date just take it straight down their throat without much chewing, similar to how you take a Jell-O shot! And thus, a high-class, vegetarian version of the college party staple was born.

Get that vodka in the freezer. It doesn't technically have to be cold for this to set but I think it helps. While that chills . . .

Put lychee juice in a small pot and bring it to a boil, then stir in your agar-agar. Let it boil for a minute before turning off the heat. Mix in your cold vodka, then pour them into whatever mold you want. I found a nice sphere mode in the candy-making section of a craft store, but you could even use an ice cube tray. Stick it in the fridge overnight to set. If you don't have all night, make sure they're in the fridge for at least an hour.

For the mignonette, simply combine the ingredients. The splash of vodka is optional, but I think it gives it that little extra bite like the traditional champagne vinegar would. Dab a small spoonful over your "lychee" and down the hatch.

A little half-shell action before a little half-dressed action.

Saffron 75

Makes 1 cocktail

For the Saffron Gin
MAKES ENOUGH FOR 6 DRINKS
12 ounces gin
Big pinch of saffron threads

For the Cocktail
2 ounces Saffron Gin
½ ounce lemon juice
½ ounce simple syrup
2 to 3 ounces champagne
Lemon twist for garnish

Some might say that saffron is an aphrodisiac simply because it's considered to be so expensive, and nice things turn people on. Others can trace it back to the days of Cleopatra when she would bathe in saffron-infused milk to increase her libido. And those nerds in the room will probably push up their glasses and spout that a 2019 study shows that saffron helped in improving sexual dysfunction. And how could it not?

Have you ever thought about what a saffron thread is? It's the stigma of a beautiful flower called the *Crocus sativus.* That's right. It's the little fuzzy center that helps catch the pollen. That's not just a pinch of saffron, that's a whole bouquet of reproductive systems . . . .

That sounded sexier in my head.

Regardless, even if the aphrodisiac effect of it all is only in our heads, infusing gin with saffron gives this drink the most stunning gold color, which is sure to bring out the flecks in your eyes, or whatever corny line you want to feed your date. Just a heads-up, while you will need only a pinch of the saffron threads, you will need three hours to let it infuse.

To infuse your gin with saffron, combine the gin and saffron in an airtight container (preferably glass) and store in the dark. Ideally, steep it for at least 3 hours (no more than 12), but be sure to give it a few shakes along the way. When it's ready, strain out the threads.

In a shaker full of ice, combine 2 ounces of the now-infused gin, lemon juice, and simple syrup. Shake cold before pouring into a flute or coupe. Top with champagne and garnish with a twist.

Just like your sheets, this saffron gin is all about the thread count.

The Best Damn Olives You've Ever Had

Serves 4

1 orange
1½ cups Castelvetrano olives
½ cup really good olive oil
1 tablespoon fennel seeds
1 tablespoon fresh rosemary
1 garlic clove, sliced
Pinch of red pepper flakes

When the movie *Clueless* came out, there were a lot of things that the character Cher Horowitz did that I wasn't down with. Mainly, dating her former brother-in-law. Although to be fair, he was played by Paul Rudd. There are few things I wouldn't do with Paul Rudd.

One thing she did do that my preteen, boy-obsessed brain took note of was to give some pretty good tips on flirting. She gave the advice, "Anything you can do to draw attention to your mouth is good." That's why we are making small, buttery Castelvetrano olives that we have to suck the pit out of. Not only do they balance hormones and improve blood flow to some, dare I say, erogenous zones . . . but they draw attention to your mouth as you take out the cleaned pit.

Preheat the oven to 400°F. Using a veggie peeler, take off about half the orange's zest in big swaths. Then use a knife to julienne until you've got a ¼ cup or so of matchstick-width orange zest.

Toss the zest, olives, olive oil, fennel seeds, rosemary, garlic, and red pepper flakes in a baking dish (making sure to evenly coat all the ingredients in your olive oil) and pop in the oven for 30 minutes; 15 minutes in, squeeze on the juice of half your orange and give everything in the dish a toss. You'll be left with salty, buttery, briny, bite-sized beauties. Be sure to warn your date there are pits. The Heimlich maneuver can be quite sexy, but let's not risk it.

Bonus: A little olive oil on your hands is perfect in case a spontaneous massage breaks out.

Big Poppy Cups

Serves 4

For the Poppy Dressing
½ cup white sugar
¼ cup olive oil
½ cup white or champagne
  vinegar
2 tablespoons minced shallot
2 tablespoons poppy seeds,
  more if desired
1 tablespoon Dijon mustard

For the Salad
Head of iceberg lettuce
A dozen or so strawberries
Pickled Onions (page 228)
Crumbled Gorgonzola
Coconut Bacon (page 228)

Salad has to be the least sexy thing to eat on a date. The way my jaw practically dislocates when I try to get a piece of frisée into my mouth is the ultimate mood killer. And because I need my jaw in perfect health for . . . other things on date night, we are going petite with our salad course. So much so that it's handheld (see the photo on page 70).

The sweetness of the strawberries, the funk of the Gorgonzola, and the crunch of the libido-increasing poppy seeds make this the perfect produce bite to rationalize the subsequent meal made of dips.

All you do for the dressing is mix all the ingredients together. You can blend it. Shake it. Twist it. Bop it. I like just enough poppy seeds to get a little texture without testing positive for opium, but feel free to add more or less to your taste and be sure to have a toothpick on standby.

Peel back the leaves of your iceberg, being careful not to rip them, so they hold their bowl shape. I like to layer at least two so the bottom doesn't fall out and you've got a lap full of salad. Once that's done, stack the rest of the ingredients as you please and drizzle with the poppy dressing.

Figs in a Blanket

Serves 4

One 14-ounce box puff pastry,
   thawed to directions
4 large Mission figs or whatever
   type you like
2 tablespoons honey
1 tablespoon red wine vinegar
1 cup pecans, finely chopped
1 tablespoon fresh thyme leaves
½ teaspoon red pepper flakes
Salt
Pepper
Crumbled feta or goat cheese
1 egg, beaten

I can't believe I'm going to say this, but I'm referencing life advice from *Clueless* one more time! I truly never knew this movie had this much impact on me. In this case, it's when Cher is getting ready for a date to come over. She tells the audience that they should always have something baking. And she wasn't wrong. It's an olfactory mood-setter; a nudge to their nose that says, *Pssst, I'm interested*.

We are baking figs, which are an aphrodisiac not only because of all the beta-carotene, which helps produce sexual hormones, and all the amino acids, which promotes stamina, but also because they just look sexy (see the photo on page 70).

Preheat the oven to 400°F. Roll out the thawed puff pastry, then cut into 16 little triangles, about 2½ inches per side. There will be extra pastry left over so you can always double the recipe or save it for another time!

Quarter your figs. In a small bowl, whisk together the honey, vinegar, pecans, thyme, red pepper flakes, and a good twist of salt and pepper. Spoon a teaspoon or so of this pecan mixture into the center of the puff pastry triangle, then top with a small chunk of cheese. Lay one fig quarter on top of the cheese and wrap the pastry around it, pressing to seal. Think of the puff pastry as a tiny robe draped seductively around the fig. Or the big, burly butter pastry hunk wrapping his arms around this dainty quartered fruit.

Brush the puff pastry with egg wash before popping your tiny, tucked-in figgies on a pan. I use parchment paper on the pan just to save cleanup for any honey leaks. Put in the oven for 20 to 25 minutes, until golden and adorable.

Braised Artichokes with Mint and Chili

Serves 4

3 large artichokes
1 lemon
3 tablespoons butter
1 tablespoon olive oil
1 shallot, thinly sliced
2 garlic cloves, chopped
2 cups dry white wine
2 cups vegetable stock
1 cup mint, chopped
½ cup Calabrian chilies, chopped
  (optional)
Lots of salt
Lots of cracked pepper

Ya'll ever get so mad at your lover that you turn them into an artichoke? No? Well, while this might not be relatable content for us mere mortals, but that's exactly what ol' playboy Zeus did. That God fell in love with a human named Cynara, and when she grew tired of her goddess life and wanted to visit her family, Zeus got so mad he turned her into an artichoke! Ummm, Zeus? Toxic masculinity much? But the artichoke lore doesn't stop there . . .

Back in the day, specifically in 16th-century Europe, artichokes were thought to make women so sexually revved up that they were banned from eating them. And while I think that was a little extreme (god forbid, a horny woman!), I do think they are a very sexy food. The way you have to get in there with your hands. The scraping of the leaf against your teeth to get the meat off. The ripping out the meaty prize of the heart like it's a finishing move in *Mortal Kombat*. It's barbaric . . . in a good way.

This edible thistle is a sex-drive missile.

The first thing you want to do is get a big bowl of water, enough that all three artichokes will fit inside. Zest your lemon and set the zest to the side before squeezing the juice of the whole lemon into the water. This will act as a bath to stop any oxidation. Take your artichoke and cut off the top ½ inch before snipping off any unattractive leaf tips. Use a vegetable peeler to take off the most fibrous outer layer of the stem, then cut your chokes in half. Do you see that fuzzy part by the heart? Use a spoon to scrape out, then give a little rinse to make sure there aren't any lingering.

As your artichoke halves bob in the lemon water, take a large pot with a lid and add your butter and oil to it over medium–low heat and add the butter and oil. Once that's melted, add your shallots and garlic and cook for a minute before adding the wine, stock, and lemon zest. Turn to low heat and let simmer for 2 to 3 minutes before adding the artichokes. Your chokes should be covered with liquid so if the pot is extra wide or you've got massive chokes, add more

veggie stock so they are submerged. Put on the lid and let it go for 20 minutes.

You'll know it's done when the leaves pull off without hesitation and you can easily scrape off the meat with your teeth. If it's fibrous, it needs to cook more. I tend to think you can undercook artichokes, but it's hard to overcook. If the liquid is too low, add a little more stock or wine. All chokes are different, so listen to yours.

Once they are done, remove the chokes and place them on a serving dish before spooning over some of the remaining cooking liquid and all the tasty shallots. I wait till this step to add salt and pepper because you never know how much your braising liquid will reduce and concentrate in saltiness. Sprinkle with mint for a pop of freshness (save a little as breath freshener) and chilies if you want to get the blood pumping!

Thank the stars these things aren't illegal!

Miso Bagna Cauda

Serves 4

2 large garlic bulbs
½ cup olive oil
Salt
Pepper
½ cup cannellini beans, rinsed
½ cup unsalted butter
1 tablespoon white miso
1 tablespoon capers, drained
¼ cup chopped parsley

Traditional Dippers

Blanched asparagus
Hearty lettuces that can
  withstand heat, such as endive
Sliced fennel
Bell pepper
Radishes

Bagna cauda, which translates to "hot bath," is a traditional dip from northern Italy. Now, according to lots of movies, taking a bath with a partner is highly erotic. I disagree. In my experience, it's awkward, cramped, and, two seconds in, I'm judging the cleanliness of my grout. Luckily, with this hot bath, it's less about getting clean and more about getting those hands dirty.

This dish is salty and garlicky and has lots of umami. Plus, despite the fact you'll have to sneak off to the bathroom and brush your teeth, garlic is a very powerful aphrodisiac. It's also very fun to sing *bagna cauda* to the tune of Heart's 1977 hit "Barracuda." That'll definitely turn your date on.

First, let's roast our garlic. Preheat the oven to 400°F. Chop off the top inch of the garlic bulbs. Then rub the now-exposed cloves with a little olive oil and a crack of salt and pepper. Wrap each bulb in a square of foil, like they are little silver baseballs. Make sure they are fully enclosed so nothing can leak out and stick them in the oven for 20 minutes.

Once roasted, get the cloves out. Now, a lot of cooking videos show people manhandling roasted garlic, squeezing the bulb like a tube of toothpaste. However, I think that leaves a lot of garlicky goodness still in the papery bulb. I prefer to pop them out and into a small bowl. In the same bowl, throw in your cannellini beans, then mash them together with a fork to make a paste.

Heat up the olive oil and butter in a small saucepan or, if you are doing it fondue style, in the pot you are planning to serve it in. Once it's heated, add the miso, capers, and parsley with a few cracks of black pepper. Let it simmer for 2 minutes before adding the garlic and bean paste. Give it a big stir.

Dip away with all your accoutrements, and, when you're done, remember that there is no bond more sacred than two people who can swig mouthwash together.

Cheddar and Stout Boozy Fondoozy

Serves 4

For the Fondue

2-pound block of sharp cheddar (ideally Irish)
1 tablespoon flour
3 tablespoons butter
1 garlic clove, minced
2 cups Guinness or other stout, more stout if needed (or milk or veggie stock)
1 tablespoon Dijon
2 tablespoons Worcestershire
A couple of splashes of your favorite hot sauce
Pinch of nutmeg

Things to Dip

Bread
Blanched veggies
Pickles
Sliced apples (a must!)

Normally, I wouldn't suggest a vat of dairy for a date night, but you must make an exception for fondue. It's quintessential sexy-time snacking. Whether you're fresh off the slopes and warming by the fire of a ski chalet . . . or you just have too much leftover cheese and need to clean that drawer out, fondue is the ultimate meal for two.

I suggest investing in a fondue set. I have had mine for years and it's always a party pleaser. But if that's not on your radar, simply make it in your most sultry saucepot. Then break out your cutest trivet stand, so you can set the pot on the table for dipping. Because the fondue stays in the pot, you can do a midmeal reheat whenever you need it.

First, grate the cheese. Y'all, this makes all the difference. Pre-shredded cheese is covered in glucose (and more) to keep it from sticking together. But that bites you in the ass when you want it to melt and come together. Grate your own! In a bowl, toss together the grated cheese with the flour.

In your fondue vessel, melt the butter and add the garlic. Once it's sweated (1 to 2 minutes), add the stout and Dijon and let it simmer for another 2 minutes to cook out some of the alcohol. When it's warm, slowly add the cheese, bit by bit, stirring consistently. If there isn't enough moisture, add a little more beer or a little milk or veggie stock. So what, who cares?

When you've added it all and it's reached peak creaminess, mix in the Worcestershire, hot sauce, and nutmeg and simmer for another 5 minutes, then serve. Deck that goodness out with bread, veggies, and pickles, but don't forget the sliced apples. They're perfect with the cheddar and full of polyphenols that stimulate blood to your . . .

May your cheddar be as sharp as Cupid's arrow.

"Just the Tips" Strawberry Martini

Makes 1 cocktail

For the Vanilla Bean Vodka
MAKES ENOUGH FOR 8 DRINKS
16 ounces vodka
2 long, fresh vanilla beans
A lot of patience

For the Strawberry Puree
2 cups strawberries
1 tablespoon sugar
1 tablespoon lemon juice
1 tablespoon water

For the Martini
White chocolate chips for the rim
2 ounces fresh Vanilla Bean Vodka
½ ounce crème de cacao (clear)
½ ounce white chocolate liqueur
  or almond Irish cream
½ ounce strawberry puree

If there were two things child-me thought were the epitome of adult and sexy, besides the occasional Frederick's of Hollywood mailer I would catch a glimpse of in our mailbox . . . they would be chocolate-covered strawberries (sometimes in tuxedoes!) and French manicures. I vividly remember going to a nail salon and seeing a poster of a woman with a French manicure dipping a strawberry into white chocolate. *Now, that's class!* I thought. I couldn't wait to be grown up, rocking French tips, buying fancy berries, and wearing what I now know is cheap lingerie!

I was a weird kid. And it was the '80s.

Now that I'm older, I can't wear acrylics because I know I would never stop flourishing my hands. I once rocked some press-ons at my friend's wedding and couldn't stop voguing and touching things like I was a hand model on QVC. But I can drink! So we are making a chocolate-covered strawberry martini that looks like the manicure of my dreams!

For the vanilla bean vodka, OF COURSE you can just buy vanilla vodka and lie that you infused it. However, if you have the forethought to make it, it takes all of 2 minutes of prep and you can tell a difference. Like the difference between a high-end perfume and a cheap body spray. Simply slit the vanilla beans down the middle lengthwise and put them with the vodka in an airtight glass container. Store it somewhere dark for at least a week, giving it a little shake every couple of days.

For the puree, be sure to cut the stems off the strawberries before tossing them, the sugar, and lemon juice in a high-power blender and go to town on it till it's smooth. You can always add a splash of water if necessary. Then strain the blend through a sieve to get the seeds out of the way. Voila! Strawberry puree. This can be done ahead of time as it will hold in the fridge for 4 to 5 days.

For the martini rim, temper the white chocolate chips either in a double broiler or the microwave and dip the rim of your glassware in it. Put them in the fridge to both harden and chill the glass as you . . .

Add your measurements of vanilla bean vodka, crème de cacao, white chocolate liqueur, and puree in a shaker full of ice. Shake, shake, shake, and then pour into your gorgeous white chocolate–rimmed glass.

Morning-After Fill:
Don't Dump Me Dumpling Soup

Serves 2

Leftovers
2 tablespoons Miso Bagna Cauda (page 79)
2 cups mix of chopped hearts from Braised Artichokes with Mint and Chili (page 76), blanched asparagus and other veggies from Miso Bagna Cauda (page 79)
1 cup (ish) diced Cheddar and Stout Boozy Fondoozy (page 80; it will be solid but will get gooey in the broth)

New Ingredients
Olive oil
1 cup pre-cut mirepoix (see Extra Tip)
2 tablespoons Italian seasoning
32 ounces veggie stock
16 ounces water
Pepper (optional)
Hot sauce (optional)
Wonton wrappers
Chopped fresh herbs (optional)

Extra Tip
If you want to prepare the mirepoix yourself because the date went bad and you can blame the tears in your eyes on chopping onion, be my guest! But otherwise, take the shortcut. Every produce aisle has a pre-cut mix, and taking that off your to-do list will make sure this soup only takes 10 minutes to prep.

After a heavy night of lots of sips and salty dips . . . I want something light the next day. A healing broth to say, "Hey, bitch! Wake up. There's still another human in your bed." This soup is kind of a play on tortellini with a dash of Italian wedding soup. Whether you want to hold a leftover artichoke like a bouquet and pretend to walk down the aisle in front of your date is totally up to you.

In a large pot, add a big ol' drizzle of olive oil over medium heat. Add the mirepoix, Italian seasoning, and 2 tablespoons of Miso Bagna Cauda to really amp the flavor. Sweat everything for 3 to 5 minutes, giving the occasional stir before adding in the veggie stock. Add the water. Bring to a boil and then turn down to a simmer.

Make them dumplings! Toss the 2 cups of whatever leftover veggies you choose and the concealed fondue into a food processor and give it a whirl. That's right—this is going to be a cheesy dumpling in the soup! Scoop a tablespoon or so of this leftover mixture onto a wonton wrapper, fold over, rub the edge of the wonton with water and then pinch the edges. They might come out looking like perfect dumplings you'd get from takeout, or they might look like reject raviolis, but they will taste just the same.

After your broth has simmered for a bit and you are liking the taste (Does it need more bagna? More pepper? Some hot sauce?), drop your dumplings in. They will need only about 3 minutes. Take off the heat, garnish with any fresh herbs you have, and you're ready to heal thyself.

SOUTHERN TAPAS

Sometimes I want my tea sweet and my dishes petite. These are down-home delicacies that feature small plates with big flavors.

When people think of Southern food, they more than likely think of massive servings. Paper plates piled so high that the bottom gets all soggy. But I think Southern food can be dainty. Handheld. Packed up into a charming little picnic and enjoyed while sitting under a magnolia tree. Like a refined British high tea, except in ours, we are making that tea full of bourbon and a few more twists. Many of these recipes are even better when you make them a day ahead, which is perfect because no one wants to see their host sweating from stress.

Slap on your finest hat and Easter gloves and go bless some hearts.

RECIPES

Classic Boiled Peanuts

Serves 4

**2 to 3 pounds raw peanuts
  (with the shell)
Water
½ cup kosher salt**

This recipe is wonderful because you must make it the day before. It's great for checking off your party to-do list, but it's also annoying because you actually have to remember to start it the day before . . .

Whenever I was on a road trip as a kid, I was always on the hunt for a handwritten cardboard sign advertising an upcoming roadside stand. The signs would usually say "fresh peaches," and then a mile closer you'd see they also have summer tomatoes or local honey. But the jackpot was when I finally laid my eyes on the magical words: "hot boiled peanuts." Boiled peanuts! They were always served in a big Styrofoam cup fit for a fountain soda, and you got another cup for your discarded shells. It was salty heaven! A Southern delicacy.

Later in life, I moved to the big cities and couldn't find them anywhere. What to do? In my case, it was fall in love with a guy from Georgia who surprises me with a pot of boiled peanuts every few months. But if your local market is fresh out of mustachioed men named Chip, here's a recipe. First, you need raw peanuts. Raw, meaning they haven't been roasted. In North Carolina, you can buy raw peanuts in the produce aisle. Nowadays, I seek them out at health stores or Asian markets. Failing that, old Amazon comes in clutch when the peanut cravings strikes.

The first step starts the night before. You need to soak your nuts (heh heh heh). Just use whichever pot you are going to end up cooking them in, be it a large pot with a lid on the stove or, my fave, a crockpot. Try and get them fully submerged with water, which can be tricky with these guys. My go-to is a plate on top, stacked with a couple of coffee cups to weigh it down. Like a homemade hydraulic press. Wish them sweet dreams and let them reconstitute overnight.

The next morning, you're going to want to get these guys cooking. I drain the overnight liquid and put in fresh water. Make sure there's enough water to cover the nuts. It's going to reduce, so be generous. Add the salt, then put the pot on the stove for at least 3 hours to boil. Test along the way. If your peanuts are totally tender, keep going! There's no overcooking them, in my opinion, but nothing worse than an al dente boiled peanut.

Sidenote

Three pounds might sound like a lot, but it's a must. Boiled peanuts are even better the next day cold right out of the fridge. Also, I go a little lighter on the salt so that guests who prefer Cajun seasoning or Old Bay can add it to their own without having to overpower all that salt. Kind of like popcorn, you can season however you see fit.

Once they're done, the final step is to find a Southerner to show you how to crack into them. The real ones will go back and chew on the shell for more brine. You can store the boiled peanuts in the fridge for up to a week, but trust me, they'll get eaten before that.

Pickled Pink Eggs

Serves 4

4 to 6 hard-boiled eggs, peeled
1 cup beet juice (you can get this
**   from a 15-ounce can)**
1 cup white sugar
¾ cup apple cider vinegar
10 whole cloves
2 bay leaves
2 tablespoons dried, yellow
**   mustard seeds**
½ tablespoon salt

I love a dusty gas station. Camo hats. Beer koozies that have jokes like "How do you get a farm girl to like you? A tractor." The only problem is that the snacks I want to eat in these places scare the hell out of me. The biggest culprit . . . pickled eggs. How many years has that massive jar of pickled eggs been sitting there? And you are out of your mind if you think someone hasn't reached in there with their bare hand! Add that to the fact that they'd always be sitting beside a jar full of pickled pigs' feet, and your girl was out. That counter felt more *Ripley's Believe It or Not!* than a place for a tasty treat. For these reasons, I never tried a pickled egg till I was well into my thirties and had fully repressed the gas station memory. Now, I'm not only obsessed with their taste, but they are the prettiest dang things you can put on a plate.

Plus, you get these little pickled mustard seeds that look like yellow caviar on top and provide a much-needed crunch. Sometimes, I make a small jar of these seeds just to have on deck, and I'm guessing now you will too.

Yes, I said "hard-boiled" and didn't give instructions for that because everyone has their own way of doing it and yours is the best. Take those eggs and place them in a sealable vessel. This could be a big ol' glass jar with a lid, or even Tupperware.

Combine the beet juice, sugar, apple cider vinegar, cloves, bay leaves, mustard seeds, and salt in a saucepan over medium heat and simmer for 5 to 7 minutes.

Now, some people pour the hot liquid all over the eggs, but I feel like it gives a weird texture! To avoid that, let it cool. Then strain the liquid into the egg jar. Why? Because you want to retain the pickled mustard seeds. I pick out the cloves and the bay leaves so that I'm left with caviar-looking texture nuggets. I like to use these as a garnish, so I store them in a separate small container in the fridge until I'm ready to use them. Let the eggs marinate for at least 3 hours but ideally overnight and prepare for a pink, pickled party in your mouth.

Goodbye Earl

Makes 1 cocktail

For the Earl Grey Bourbon
MAKES ENOUGH FOR 8 DRINKS
16 ounces bourbon
4 bags of Earl Grey tea

For the Cocktail
2 ounces Earl Grey Bourbon
1 ounce lemon juice
1 ounce honey simple syrup
Lemon and a really good
  maraschino cherry for garnish

When I found out my beloved bergamot looked like a wrinkly lime, I was shocked. I don't know what I was expecting. A spice? A leafy herb? As for my attraction to Earl Grey tea, it suddenly made sense. I'm a self-proclaimed "citrus slut," so it's no wonder I gravitated toward the lemon and bitter orange flavorings of Earl Grey, which is scented with bergamot oil.

This drink was created when hanging out at a cooking retreat with one of my Southern chef heroes, Vivian Howard. I was making cocktails for all the ladies attending and had come up with this concoction, simply calling it an Earl Grey Old-Fashioned or something basic like that. But after a night out on Bald Head Island where the whole gang scream-sang "Goodbye Earl" by the Chicks at a karaoke bar, I had found a name.

This drink might look soft, but it'll knock you on your ass like you're drinking on rollerblades. So, if you want to temper it, top with club soda.

Put your bourbon in a big mason jar and drop in the tea bags. I like to steep this for 2½ to 3 hours. Unlike some more floral teas, Earl Grey can turn bitter quickly if steeped too long. Once it's tasting right, fish out the tea bags (with tongs, not your hands, you animal).

Sidenote
If this drink hits the flavor notes for you but is a little too strong, you can always treat it like an Arnold Palmer. That is, make your Earl Grey bourbon and top it with lemonade.

In a shaker full of ice, combine 2 ounces of the Earl Grey bourbon, lemon juice, and honey simple syrup. Shake until cold, then pour over a big ice cube. Garnish with a lemon, cherry, and the entirety of the Chicks music catalog.

Broccoli Salad Summer Rolls

Serves 4

3 cups diced broccoli
1 cup diced celery
1 cup dried cranberries, diced
1 cup fried onions (like French's
  or other store-bought)
1 cup shredded cheddar
2 tablespoons olive oil
2 tablespoons red wine vinegar
Salt
Pepper
Package of summer roll wrappers
Bowl of hot water
Poppy Dressing (page 72) or Tahini
  Sauce (page 229)

Extra Credit
Fresh violets or other edible
  flowers to make them pretty.

I love raw broccoli. I have been known to even bust into a bag of florets on the way home from the grocery store. Bless all those people who have pulled up beside at a stoplight and watched me going full petting zoo, just raw dogging broccoli like I'm a ravenous turtle.

Considering I like broccoli in its purest form, you better believe I have a soft spot for a good old-school broccoli salad. I'm talking church potluck style. Even then, it can be a little too clunky. We refine the eating process here by rolling up a salad into dainty little summer rolls. Extra points if you add violets or other edible flowers. Trust me, these will have your Southern Soiree guests putting their hands to their chest and gasping from the beauty. You might want to bring a fainting couch.

Just like a kale salad, I feel like raw broccoli needs a bit of a massage. So, in a bowl, drizzle your olive oil over the brocccoli and give it a little shiatsu! Combine the relaxed broccoli, celery, cranberries, fried onions, and cheddar with the red wine vinegar. Give a toss and add salt and pepper to taste. At this point, you've got a mayo-free broccoli salad, but we're going to make it pretty.

Lay out your rolling station. My setup is a cutting board with a tea towel spread out on it and a large bowl of hot water. You want it hot enough to soften the wrappers but not burn off your fingerprints. One by one, take a summer roll wrapper and dip it in water till it goes clear and pliable. You're going to want to hold it on either side to keep it spread. Like, if you've ever worn a sheet mask, hold it like you do when you've taken it off the plastic and are about to put it on your face. OK, your wrapper is ready. Place it on the tea towel flat, scoop on some of the broccoli salad mix (and flower, if using), spread it across the wrap, and tuck in the side and roll on up. Serve alongside your dipping sauce and feel bad that you are about to destroy your beautiful work.

Sidenote
This sturdy salad can easily retain its texture after a night in the fridge. So, if you feel like you made too much or your wrist goes on strike from rolling, simply refrigerate and eat tomorrow.

Lima Bean Hummus with Succotash Salsa

Serves 4

For the Hummus

4 cups frozen lima beans
1 cup feta
1 cup cilantro
½ cup tahini
¼ cup red wine vinegar
¼ cup olive oil
Juice of one lemon, half of its zest
2 garlic cloves
1 de-seeded jalapeño
Salt
Pepper

For the Succotash Salsa

¼ cup diced red onion
¼ cup diced pickled banana
  peppers, plus a splash of
  the brine
¼ cup feta
Dozen halved grape tomatoes

I have no idea when hummus became such an integral part of everyday snackage. I don't remember eating hummus as a child. But nowadays, you would be hard-pressed to approach a table at a party and not find at least one thing of hummus, more than likely in a tub with the brand name that rhymes with *candelabra*.

And I'm not complaining! Hummus is delectable, and a vegetarian's protein dream. However, we've got to branch out from just the chickpea. There are so many creamy legumes ready to take on the challenge, and one that I think does it perfectly is . . .

The lima bean. I've always loved limas, or butter beans, which they are also called—and which would be a perfect name for a French bulldog. Even when other kids would turn their noses up at them, I'd grab seconds. Besides being a sweet green color, they are so creamy on the inside. It's a combo that makes them perfect for a dip *and* a prank. I like to tell people it's guacamole, and then watch their faces go from horror, to confusion, then sheer delight.

This could not be easier. First, you've got to cook your limas. If you have access to fresh ones, congrats on being an actual farmer! But if you are like most of us and do not, please use frozen. They are so much fresher than canned. Cook them in boiling water till they're tender (about 5 minutes), drain, and cool.

Combine your now-cooked limas with all the other hummus ingredients in a food processor. I still like mine to have a little texture to it, but if you want it super smooth let it go longer, add a little more olive oil, lemon juice, tahini, or even a splash of water. Salt and pepper to taste.

For the salsa, toss all the salsa items together and give it a lil' splash of the brine from the banana peppers. Give your hummus a little succotash ceiling and dig in!

Yams Casino

Serves 4

3 medium sweet potatoes
Olive oil
3 tablespoons butter
2 garlic cloves, minced
½ cup minced shallot
½ cup minced green bell pepper
1 cup white wine
1 cup bread crumbs
½ cup grated Parmesan
1 cup shredded mozzarella
1 cup chopped parsley
½ cup Coconut Bacon (page 228)
Sour cream

OK, fine! You got me. We are using sweet potatoes and calling them yams. Before you sick the tuber police on me, I know they aren't the same thing. But they are pretty close, and this pun was too good to pass up! You see, the term "clams casino" has always made me picture an old lady clam sitting at a slot machine, smoking a cigarette, and drinking a martini. One day, I want that image on a T-shirt. Dream big, Mamrie!

This dish is essentially the love child of the famous seafood appetizer and a loaded potato skin. Beyond all that, it's just delicious and sitting down to a plate of these will make you feel like you hit the jackpot!

Give the sweet potatoes a few good stabs with a fork, then rub them with olive oil. Place them in a 425°F oven. I put them directly on the rack. These should take around 45 minutes, depending on size.

Take out the cooked sweet potatoes and let them cool. Once you can handle them safely, slice them all the way in half, then use a spoon to scoop out the flesh, leaving about a ¼-inch of potato padding. Like little sweet potato bowls. Save those insides for Sweet Potato Tortillas on page 105.

In a large skillet, melt the butter over medium–low heat before adding the garlic, shallots, and bell pepper. Cook for about 5 minutes until the shallots are translucent. Add the white wine and let the booze cook out, simmering for about 2 minutes. Take off the heat and add in your bread crumbs, Parmesan, mozzarella, parsley, and crumbled coconut bacon.

Evenly spoon the casino mixture over the sweet potato skins. Bake at 350°F for 10 minutes. Take out of the oven and drizzle with sour cream.

Heirlooms with Down-Home Dukkah

Serves 4

For the Dukkah
1 cup pecans
¼ cup white sesame seeds
1 tablespoon cumin seeds
1 tablespoon coriander seeds
1 tablespoon fennel seeds
½ teaspoon cayenne
½ tablespoon brown sugar
Flaky salt

For the Tomatoes
The juiciest tomatoes you can get
your hands on
Balsamic vinegar (optional)

If the tomatoes are popping, you don't need to do much to them. Summertime for me means slicing into a perfectly ripe tomato, giving it some salt and pepper, and digging right in. That is, until I decided to get crazy one day and sprinkle on a little dukkah. If you've never had dukkah, congrats, your life is about to be different now. It's a perfect mix of spices and crushed nuts that gives a pop of texture needed on so many dishes.

While our dukkah is going the traditional route with fennel and sesame seeds, we are also bringing in the lord of the Southern nut, pecans. No matter how you pronounce *pecan,* it makes the perfect addition to your new favorite spice blend.

In a medium skillet over medium heat, toast the pecans for 3 minutes or so. Let cool, then chop incredibly fine or pulse in a food processor. You want the pieces to be about the size of sunflower seeds.

Then you're going to want to toast all your sesame, cumin, coriander, and fennel seeds just the same way. Use the same skillet. It ain't dirty! Be careful not to let them burn. All you're wanting to do here is get them to release their oil. Once toasted, grind them up with a mortar and pestle and allow time to cool. If you don't have a mortar and pestle, just stick them in a zip-top bag and beat the hell out of it. Mix with the cayenne, nuts, brown sugar, and a few good pinches of flaky salt.

Slice your heirlooms all pretty like. I like mine with a splash of balsamic vinegar and then a generous coating of the dukkah. Dig in.

An Egyptian spice that makes everything nice.

Watergate Martini

Makes 1 cocktail

2½ ounces white rum
1 ounce pineapple juice
½ ounce pistachio liqueur or
   pistachio syrup for coffee
Whipped cream for garnish
1 bright red cherry for garnish

No, this is not the part of the book where I tell you I am obsessed with the 1972 scandal that ultimately led to President Nixon's resignation. It is, however, the part of the book where I once again create a cocktail inspired by a very '70s-style salad. The term "salad" is definitely used loosely, considering that this thing is top-to-bottom sweet. There is not a whisper of lettuce to be seen.

So, where did the Watergate salad originate from? Y'all, I did the research but what I found left me even more confused. There are tons of theories, even a fun fact that Helen Keller (yes, that Helen Keller) submitted it in 1922 to a cookbook featuring recipes from famous people. What?! If reading this sentence made you want a drink, join the club and grab a glass.

This cocktail is essentially a pistachio and pineapple dessert sipper. There are a few brands that do indeed make a pistachio liqueur, but I found that pistachio syrup made for coffees works just as well (like Monin or Torani). In fact, I brought a bottle of pistachio syrup to the photoshoot for the drink pictured here, and a month later my photographer and friend, Claire, was still mixing it into her cappuccino every morning. So it definitely won't go to waste.

Shake everything except the garnishes together in a shaker full of ice, then pour into the coldest coupe possible. Swirl that whipped cream high, top with the cherry, then tell everyone that Hellen Keller fact.

More desserts need to be called salad. Cheesecake salad? Banana split salad? I love the '70s.

Morning-After Fill: Sweet Potato Tortilla Breakfast Tacos

Serves 2

Leftovers

1 cup leftover sweet potato, mashed from Yams Casino (page 99)

1 cup Lima Bean Hummus with Succotash Salsa (page 98)

½ cup diced tomatoes from Heirlooms with Down-Home Dukkah (page 100)

Sprinkle of Coconut Bacon (page 228)

Broccoli Salad Summer Roll filling (page 94; optional)

New Ingredients

1¼ cups all-purpose flour, more if needed

1 teaspoon salt

1 teaspoon cumin

Big pinch of chili powder

1 tablespoon olive oil

4 eggs

Cheese of choice for garnish

Have you ever avoided someone because they looked incredibly intimidating and then when you finally spoke to them, you realized they were super chill and nice? That is how I would describe my relationship with homemade tortillas.

They always seem so hard! They come with their own gadget, after all. Whenever you see someone making tortillas from scratch, it's usually at a taco cart in Mexico City. They are always pressed by a woman who has been doing this for decades. I assumed there was no way I could make them in my own kitchen . . . but I was wrong!

The truth is, they are so simple to make. A couple of ingredients and a dash of courage and you're toasting up tortillas in no time. And the best part is that you don't have to ever admit how easy they are to make. Let your guests take out the trash or wash the dishes—all the stuff you don't want to do—while you "sweat" over the stove.

You know the saying "Fake it till you make it"? That's kind of what you need to do with this. Get your role play on. In a bowl, use your hands to mix the flour, sweet potato mash, salt, cumin, and chili powder. If it feels too sticky, you can add a little more flour. Once it's combined, form it into one big ball (like they do with bread on the *Bake Off* show) and just set it aside for 3 minutes or so.

OK. Moment of truth. Flour your surface (counter or big cutting board) and roll out your dough into a big log before cutting into 8 pieces and then rolling those pieces into their own little balls. Then flatten these out into tortillas with a rolling pin, or get yourself a tortilla press, which are incredibly affordable and now that you're a tortilla whiz, you'll use all the time. Roll or press out your tortillas to about a ¼ inch or so.

Heat the olive oil in a medium pan (or skip the oil and use a nonstick pan) over medium heat, then cook the tortillas for about 2 minutes on each side.

Choose your own adventure from here. I like to give a schmear of the lima dip. Put on some sliced tomatoes, then top with scrambled eggs with cheese and coconut bacon. If you want a little more greens up in there, you can sauté your leftover broccoli salad. The possibilities are endless.

Send pics to all your friends to boast that you made your own tortillas.

CHEF'S KISS

My favorite renditions
of Italian classics that you
won't want to give the boot.

My love for Italian food burns strong, and has since I was but a wee little idiot. It was a safe place. There are always pasta dishes without meat, so I knew I could order without there being a big fuss. Give me fettuccine, not people fretting to make sure I got enough to eat! I want puttanesca, not putting-up-unnecessary-stress-a! (That one was a stretch.) It's this simple convenience that made Italian food the go-to in my teen years. And it's why, in high school, I always suggested we venture to the mecca of small-town marinara for every special Friday.

Yes, I'm talking about the one and only . . . Olive Garden.

If you went to high school in the late '90s or early 2000s, then I'm sure you know what I mean. Olive Garden was a celebration station, be it for a friend's birthday, a fancy meal before a dance, an anniversary date. Sure, Macaroni Grill had those paper table covers we could draw on, and the occasional musical theater major would come by our table and belt out "That's Amore," but Olive Garden was the ultimate. They grated their cheese tableside! And my cocky fourteen-year-old ass would let them grate that cheese till they broke a sweat.

But since those days of feasting on unlimited pasta bowls and spraining waiter's wrists, I have had the pleasure of visiting Italy a few times. My Italian palate grew accordingly, and I discovered you can get a lot of dishes and ingredients in the motherland that, shocker, aren't on the menu of a massive American chain restaurant. This chapter is a combo of highbrow and lowbrow. From bright fennel salads to my riff on SpaghettiOs, it covers my love of Italian food from authentic to "aw, that's not even close."

RECIPES

Caprese Collins

Makes 1 cocktail

For the Tomato Water
MAKES ENOUGH FOR 4 TO 6 DRINKS
1½ pounds big, ripe tomatoes
1½ teaspoons salt

For the Cocktail
2 basil leaves
2 ounces gin
2 ounces Tomato Water (from above)
1 ounce lemon juice
½ ounce simple syrup

Garnish
Toothpick
Bocconcini
Basil leaf
Grape tomato

I love a caprese. Eating a softball's worth of mozzarella but calling it a salad since you added a few basil sprigs and tomato slices is genius. It's like calling an apple pie a green juice because there are a few pounds of fruit in it.

This drink pays homage to this salad imposter by using a crisp, light tomato water. For decades, if you wanted a drink to have a tinge of tomato, your brain went to a Bloody Mary, which I have always considered more of a breakfast smoothie than a cocktail. Lucky for us, tomato water started popping up in all the fancy cocktail publications. And while some methods get the liquid completely clear, I like the sligggghtest bit of pulp to keep some color. And while the only cheese in this drink is the garnish, you are going to need a cheesecloth.

For the tomato water: Roughly chop the tomatoes, being sure to save the juice. Sprinkle with the salt and let sit for 10 minutes before blending. Take your blended tomatoes and strain through a cheesecloth. This is important! Not just a fine mesh, get yourself a $2 cheesecloth at the grocery store. What you're left with is a translucent, fragrant water full of tomato flavor.

For the cocktail: Put the basil leaves in the shaker and muddle the heck out of them to release all the fragrant, fresh oils. Add the gin, tomato water, lemon juice, and simple syrup with ice and shake it up, baby!

Strain into a glass, either on a big ice cube or up, then garnish with a little caprese toothpick; I spear on a piece of bocconcini, a basil leaf, and a grape tomato.

Technically a Virgin Martini

Makes 1 cocktail

For the Olive Oil–Washed Vodka
MAKES ENOUGH FOR 8 DRINKS
2 cups vodka
½ cup good extra-virgin olive oil

For the Martini
2 ounces Olive Oil–Washed Vodka
½ ounce dry vermouth
Olive for garnish

We all have those culinary moments that haunt us. Like when you accidentally added a buttload of cayenne to your chili thinking it was paprika, and now your friends' mouths are on fire. Or you realized those brownies that just went in the oven definitely have two cups of salt in them, not sugar. For me, it was one day when my friend and I were about to throw a Bloody Mary party. We slaved over the mix. Pressed our own tomatoes. Grated fresh horseradish. On the very last step, I thought, *This would be great with a little olive brine.*

So I grabbed a jar of olives and gave the mix a big glug of the juice before realizing, "Shit! Those were in oil, not brine." I looked down to see our bloody mix looking like a pipeline had burst. I tried to use spoons, then napkins to siphon off the oil on top, but it was no use. The damage was done. It was a full-on disaster. The guests humored me by saying it was actually kind of good—interesting even. But the truth was obvious when they choked down half a glass out of pity and then switched to mimosas.

I had no clue that all I needed to do was stick that mix in the freezer, let it solidify, and then scoop off the oil slick. Lucky for us, I now know. And, what's more, oil-washed cocktails are all the rage these days. So, while this thing is a booze-heavy martini, those undertones of EVOO make it technically a virgin. Hell, it's an extra virgin.

For the oil-washed vodka: My basic recipe for oil washing is ½ cup of oil per 2 cups of booze. If you want more, or less, just use that ratio (½ to 2) and whirl in a blender till super incorporated. Stick that in an airtight container and put in the freezer overnight.

The next day you are met with infused vodka on the bottom and a solidified frisbee of fat on the top. Take off the fat and discard it, or throw it at an enemy. Then take the vodka and strain it through a cheesecloth (or coffee filter if you're desperate) to get out any straggler bits. Boom, olive oil–washed vodka.

Combine the 2 ounces of olive oil vodka and the vermouth in a shaker of ice. Get it good and cold and pour it into your glass. Garnish with an olive or whatever you prefer and prepare for compliments.

Fall Formaggio Ball

Serves 4

1 cup dehydrated beet chips
1 Gournay cheese ball, typically
   5 ounces (Boursin brand)
½ cup smoked blue cheese
1 cup candied walnuts
Things for dipping! I suggest
   sliced pears, beet chips, endive,
   and seeded crackers

This is an old-school cheese ball that you might have seen on a table at a party in the '80s, but classed up. Instead of cream cheese, we are using Gournay, which, in non-cheesemonger terms, is the Boursin brand you can find anywhere. The cool thing about this appetizer, besides watching your friends scoff at how retro it is before demolishing the whole thing, is that it has the flavors of an autumn salad.

Between the blue cheese, candied walnuts, and beets, this ball is a mixed field green short of being considered healthy, so go ahead and release any guilt.

Stick the beet chips in a coffee grinder or in a zip-top bag and crush the hell out of them. Now take that beet powder and whip in a bowl with your cheeses. You are left with a gorgeous pink fromage. Using your hands, form it into a ball and stick it in the fridge for a few minutes to hold the shape as you . . .

Chop the candied walnuts. You are more than welcome to make your own but I prefer to save myself a step and buy the walnuts from the store pre-candied. Roll your pink ball in the nuts. Serve with your favorite things for dipping.

When it comes to this cheese ball, think pink!

Orange and Fennel Salad with Fried Capers

Serves 4

For the Citrus Dressing
1 navel or blood orange
¼ cup olive oil
2 tablespoons lemon juice
1½ tablespoons honey
1 tablespoon Dijon
2 garlic cloves, minced
Lots of cracked pepper

For the Salad
2 navel or blood oranges
1 large fennel bulb, including
  the fronds for garnish
1 pound endive (Belgian,
  radicchio, your preference)
2 tablespoons olive oil or
  vegetable oil
2 tablespoons capers
2 to 3 cups arugula
4 to 5 large basil leaves,
  chiffonade

This recipe is not rocket science. However, arugula is called rocket in Australia, so maybe it is! This salad has all the iconic citrus and fennel vibes of a salad you can find in a café in Italy. It's bright, tart, herbaceous, and my ideal way to cleanse your palate in between pastas and pizza.

You want fresh juice for the dressing. Whether you decide to go with navel or blood oranges, take one of the oranges and juice it. Ideally, you will end up with 2 tablespoons. Mix that juice with the rest of the dressing ingredients.

For the salad: Using a mandoline, slice the fennel as thin as possible. Peel the remaining 2 oranges and chop them into chunks. If you know how to supreme citrus, by God, go for it! I don't have it in me. Roughly chop your endive.

Warm up the 2 tablespoons of olive or vegetable oil in a small pan over high heat. You'll want about an ⅛ inch in the pan. Make sure the capers are super dry, patting them down with a paper towel if needed. Once the oil is hot, toss in your capers to fry up. This should take only 2 to 3 minutes, and they will burst open and get crispy. When done, spoon them out and put on paper towel to soak up the excess oil.

Toss the endive, arugula, and fennel in some of the dressing, then plate. Remember you can add more but not take away. Arrange the oranges all around. Garnish with fennel fronds, the basil, and fried capers.

Cauliflower Bolognese Zucchini Boats

Serves 4

3 large zucchinis
Salt
2 tablespoons butter
3 garlic cloves, smashed
¼ cup celery, chopped
¼ cup onion, chopped
¼ cup carrots, chopped
4 tablespoons tomato paste
One 14-ounce can crushed
    tomatoes
1½ tablespoons dried Italian
    seasoning
Pinch of red pepper flakes
½ cup red wine
2 cups cauliflower rice
2 cups mozzarella, shredded

We all remember our first, right? Whether it was at home or a Renaissance faire, or perhaps even Panera Bread, we all remember the first time we saw a bread bowl filled with piping hot soup—a marvel of modern ingenuity. Despite wanting to use a hollowed-out loaf of sourdough as everyday plateware, my body disagrees. However, it was the gateway for my obsession with stuffing foods into other foods.

Zucchinis are perfect for this. Not only are their insides tender enough to easily scoop out, but when they are stuffed, they are called boats. How cute is that? I guess we could call ours gondolas, in honor of Italy and Venice.

Whatever water vehicle you call it, stuff it full of this cauliflower rice that's treated like a hearty Bolognese, and your guests will be happy and also stuffed.

Preheat the oven to 400°F. Slice the zucchinis lengthwise, then use your melon baller to hollow them out into a boat. Give them a sprinkle of salt. This will help bring out the moisture so by the time the Bolognese is ready, we can pat off the water that the salt pulls out. Like patting down the sweaty brow of a lover. . . . That sounded sexier in my head.

In a large pot, add the butter over medium heat. Add the garlic, celery, onion, carrots, and tomato paste. Sauté for 4 to 5 minutes. Once the onions are translucent, add the can of tomatoes, Italian seasoning, red pepper flakes, and red wine. Bring to a boil, then turn to low, and simmer for 12 to 15 minutes to reduce down a bit and to cook out the alcohol in the wine.

Stir in the cauliflower rice and let it cook for 3 to 4 minutes. You still want it a little al dente as it will continue to cook in the oven.

Scoop the cauliflower Bolognese into your zucchini boats and place on a pan or cooking dish. Scatter your mozzarella on top. Pop in the oven for 10 minutes. Bring these boats into the mouth harbor.

Extra Tip
Because we are doing equal parts celery, onion, and carrots . . . just buy store-bought mirepoix and add 1½ cups.

Cacio e Pea Peas

Serves 4

4 cups frozen green peas
Olive oil
3 tablespoons butter
2 teaspoons cracked black pepper,
  more for serving
1½ cups grated Pecorino Romano,
  more for serving
Reserved cooking water

I love cacio e pepe, but every time I make it, I end up adding peas to it. It needs a little freshness! Or maybe just adding a few spoonfuls of green in there negates the fact that I'm just eating straight-up pasta, butter, and cheese. So, I thought, why not skip the pasta and just make some cacio peas?

Now, obviously, if you have access to fresh peas, go for it (Trader Joe's is my year-round go-to for them). But if you don't have fresh peas available to you, just go with full-size frozen peas. And here's a cool thing. You know how you normally save a little pasta water to make cacio e pepe? Just like pasta, peas also release a little starch into the water. So we are gonna use that to help thicken the sauce.

Put a small pot of water over high heat, enough to cover the peas, and give a good squirt of olive oil in it. Once it comes to a boil, add your peas and cook for 3 to 4 minutes. Before you strain through a colander, save 1 to 2 cups of the cooking water.

Now that the peas are in a colander, take that same pot, because no one wants to do extra dishes, and melt the butter over low heat. Once it's melted, whisk in the pepper and let it cook for a minute, bringing out the oils of the pepper. Add in the Pecorino Romano. Give that a few stirs before slowly whisking in the reserved cooking water. You want it to be a nice glaze-like sauce.

Toss in the peas to coat in the sauce before plating up and giving it a little more cheese and pepper on top.

Drunken Os

Serves 4

**16 ounces anelli pasta, reserving
  2 cups of the pasta water
Salt
4 tablespoons butter
3 garlic cloves, minced
One small shallot, minced
2 tablespoons tomato paste
1 teaspoon red pepper flakes
¼ cup vodka
2 cups crushed tomatoes
½ cup heavy cream
1 cup Parmesan
Lots of cracked pepper, to taste**

Growing up, there were a lot of snacks and foods in the pop culture zeitgeist that I wanted to try but couldn't. Like Hamburger Helper. A glove with a face making your pasta? Count me in! Chef Boyardee seemed like a nice enough man, but all his raviolis were full of beef.

So I was amped when I found out that SpaghettiOs are vegetarian. I was so excited to warm up those saucy Os, fresh from the can, finally getting to eat something I saw on TV like the rest of America . . . . Then I tasted it. I immediately realized I wasn't missing out.

No shade to those who love it, but to me it just tasted like a factory had a surplus of tomato soup laying around and decided to chuck some pasta rings into it. Not my thing. In fact, I would have to be very drunk to eat them again.

Rather than having to get wasted to taste it (kind of rhymes), we are going to get our pasta rings drunk themselves by dunking them in a creamy, garlicky vodka sauce. Don't worry, the booze cooks out so you aren't going to get a hangover from this dish. We use O-shaped pasta to really scratch that nostalgia itch, but this would be fantastic with any shaped pasta you have on hand.

Get a big pot of water boiling for your pasta. Be sure to salt it! Cook as directed, but before you drain, be sure to save 2 cups of the starchy pasta water. You probably won't need that much but better to have, than regret. As that's bubbling away . . .

In a large sauté pan, toss in the butter over medium heat. Add the garlic and shallots and cook for 3 to 4 minutes, until they are tender. Add the tomato paste and red pepper flakes and mix everything together. Don't worry that the bright red of the tomato paste will get darker, this is supposed to happen. Cook this for 2 to 3 minutes before . . .

Add that vodka baby! It will essentially deglaze the pan. Scrape up all those bits that are sticking to the bottom. Turn the heat to low and add the crushed tomatoes and half of the reserved pasta water. Let simmer for another 2 to 3 minutes before whisking in the heavy cream and Parmesan.

Mix in your pasta! If it's feeling dry, add a little more pasta water a little bit at a time until you reach your desired sauciness. What you're left with is some grown-up SpaghettiOs and, bonus, the rest of the bottle of vodka!

Pistachio Pesto Bucatini with Lemon Ricotta

Serves 4

One 16-ounce box of bucatini or whichever pasta you want
Salt
1 cup ricotta
Lots of cracked pepper
1 tablespoon lemon zest, more if needed
Squeeze of lemon juice (optional)
Pistachio Pesto (page 228)

If I say something controversial, do you promise not to slam this book shut, burn it, or have it banned in Florida? I love pesto, but I think pine nuts aren't the right nut for it. There, I said it. Pine nuts are wonderful, are even better when they are called *pignolis*, but I like a little more texture to my pesto. Enter, the pistachios.

Pistachios are earthy with just the tiniest sweet note to them. They can stand up to the punch of basil and acidity in the pesto. They are also cheaper than pine nuts, which we love to see. This is my absolute go-to pesto and I've been converting people every chance I get. The only pitfall with pesto is that sometimes it can feel a little dry on a pasta. A little plain Jane. This is why I love adding a scoop of lemony ricotta on top. You can stir in as you go and give this dish some moisture and creaminess that it craves!

Get a big pot of water boiling for your pasta. Be sure to salt it! Cook as directed, and while that boils . . .

Put the ricotta in a bowl and mix in your lemon zest. Stir together with a pinch of salt and a ton of cracked black pepper. This is usually lemony enough for me as the pesto has lemon in it too, but taste as you go. You can always add more zest or a little squeeze of the juice itself.

Remove the pasta from the heat, drain, and return it to the pot. Gently stir in the pesto to combine. Serve in a shallow bowl or plate with a nice scoop of the lemon ricotta on top.

Coffee and Cigarettes

Makes 1 cocktail

1½ ounces vodka (see Extra Tip)
½ ounce amaro (I like Amaro
Nonino for its orange
undertones)
½ orange liqueur or Grand Marnier
Single shot of espresso
Orange twist for garnish

This picture right here is my ideal way to end a meal. Except I haven't had a cigarette in over 20 years and I'm not a huge fan of warm cocktails (besides a hot toddy when you're sick, but that's just science). As for the cigarettes part, what you're looking at here are pretzels dipped in white chocolate with crushed-up Oreos as the ashy tip. I will not be giving a recipe for that because it's so simple I think I just did.

This drink is my amaro and orange riff on an espresso martini served in an actual coffee cup. You still have the handle so you're not going to warm up the drink with your hands, and, if you've been partaking during the meal, you have less of a chance of knocking it over with your exaggerated hand gestures.

Extra Tip

Try using the vanilla bean vodka from "Just the Tips" Strawberry Martini on page 83. Also, if you don't have an espresso machine at home, all good. I keep a little jar of instant espresso on hand for a pick-me-up in my coffee when it's a rough morning, or for making a cocktail like this. Alternatively, you can stop by your local coffee shop earlier in the day and get a few long pours. Just keep it in the fridge 'til you're ready to make that cocktail.

Combine everything except the orange twist in a shaker full of ice and shake it till it's super cold. Be sure not to use freshly pulled, hot espresso or you're going to have a watered-down drink. Pour into your favorite prechilled mug and garnish with a twist of orange.

Morning-After Fill: Pastiche Quiche

Serves 4

Leftovers

**2 cups of any combo of chopped
Cauliflower Bolognese Zucchini
Boats (page 116), Pistachio Pesto
(page 228), and Cacio e Pea Peas
(page 119)**

Extra Ingredients

Pie crust
6 eggs
¾ cup milk or cream
Salt
Pepper
Grated Parmesan for topping

Leftover pasta is perfect the way it is: reheated or eaten cold with your fingers in front of an open fridge. So, our MAF isn't trying to mess with perfection. But we do have something to heal our wounds . . . a protein-packed quiche.

Quiche is one of my favorite ways to rework leftovers. It takes all of about 5 minutes to prepare and takes about half an hour in the oven, which is the perfect amount of time to get in an episode of trash TV. I call it pastiche quiche because a *pastiche* is "an artistic work in a style that imitates that of another work, artist, or period," and this work pays homage to last night's feast!

Preheat the oven to 375°F. Press your dough into a greased pie tin or, if you decide to buy a frozen one already in a tin, make sure it is thawed. Decide whichever leftovers you want in. The possibilities are endless. I like to arrange the leftovers in the pie crust almost like pizza toppings before pouring in the custard mixture to make sure everything is evenly distributed.

To make the custard mixture, whip together the eggs and milk, and give it a good salt and peppering before pouring into the pie tin. Top with a little Parmesan, then pop in the oven for 30 to 40 minutes. Use a knife to poke the center and make sure it comes out clean to see if it's ready. Remember, there is no shame in using the pie tin itself as a plate to eat an entire quiche yourself. Fewer dishes!

Sidenote

The quiche pictured is a mix of chopped Zucchini Boats (page 116) and Cacio e Pea Peas (page 119), as well as a little arugula left over from the salad, and a sliced tomato I didn't use from the Caprese Collins (page 110).

A VERY VERDURA DINNER

My love of Mexican food knows no bounds, but sometimes I need extra veggies. Grab a margarita, because I'm about to feed ya!

If you don't like Mexican food, I don't trust you. A night at a Mexican restaurant is one of life's sweetest gifts. Picture it. It's Friday at 5 p.m. and you're sitting on the patio of a Mexican restaurant. A huge margarita is placed in front of you. A salty basket of chips and fresh salsa beckons to you to dive in . . . . "You'll only have a couple," a voice in your head whispers, incorrectly. And your friend sits across from you with hot gossip as the sun sets toward your weekend with zero plans.

This is MY HEAVEN.

Except that, if we don't just stay for happy hour and let it roll into dinner, I am more than likely filling my belly with 12 servings of cheese or a bunch of beans. At best, there's probably a veggie fajita. Don't get me wrong, I love an entrée that makes an entrance, but fajitas feel less satisfying when the sizzling plate is just filled with a sad mix of onions and bell peppers. This is the vegetarian conundrum. Most of the menus at delicious Mexican joints are not brimming with options for the carne adverse. They might have a few dishes they've cobbled together with essentially the garnishes of other dishes. And a boatload of cheese.

Or, because I live in Southern California, I can go to a vegan Mexican place where everything is fake meat or tofu. Trouble is, while I don't want just a cheese enchilada at the authentic spot, I also don't need half a pound of hemp seed tofu carnitas. Just give me some actual vegetables, dammit! Enter *verduras,* which is "vegetables" in Spanish.

In this chapter, I show you some of my favorite recipes that finally scratch that itch.

Spicy Strawberry Habanero Aguachile

Serves 4

For the Marinade
4 hibiscus tea bags
1 cup boiling water
1 cup ripe strawberries, hulled
2 to 3 limes, juiced (about half
  a cup)
1 tablespoon soy sauce
1 habanero
1½ teaspoons sugar

For the Aguachile
Whatever your heart desires;
  my recs are . . .
Jicama
Cucumber
Sliced strawberries
Golden beet
Thin red onion
Cilantro
Gooseberries

Aguachile, which translates to "chili water," is a bright and refreshing kick in the jaw of flavor. It's also freaking gorgeous. The only bummer is that it is usually made with shrimp or raw fish. One time, my friend ordered it, and I was knocked out of the booth by the bright pink color. This one wasn't just the normal green aguachile, this was a strawberry aguachile that had some heat from serrano (I sipped the broth, sue me).

We are making our version by also using strawberries. But we're adding in the heat of a habanero because it plays nicely with the fruit notes of strawberry. And we're using a traditional Mexican tea, hibiscus (which they call Jamaica), as our base. Think of this like a cold starter salad, or you can chop everything much smaller and eat like a chunky fruit salad.

Extra Tip
Make a little extra of the marinade, but without the soy sauce, and set it to the side for the next morning. Mix with a little tequila over ice for some hair of the dog, and, honey, you're good as new. Basically, it's a spicy strawberry margarita. Two recipes for the price of one.

First, steep an extremely bold cup of tea to the point of being tannic. I'm talking all 4 tea bags in 1 cup of boiling water. So, if you decide to go for something besides hibiscus, all good. Just double-check that it's not one of those Smooth Move teas. Once it's brewed and at room temp, put all the marinade ingredients in a blender till smooth. I deseed my habanero before I do this, but this depends on preferred spice level. Then, either run it through a cheesecloth or fine mesh sieve several times until it's got all the debris out. Put in the fridge or freezer for a few minutes to get ice cold. Great to make ahead.

Arrange the fruit and veggie goodies in a shallow bowl or plate with a decent edge on it. Pour the aguachile broth on top. Bonus points if you do this tableside.

Oaxacan Penicillin

Makes 1 cocktail

Let's be honest, we all buy our drugs in Mexico, amiright?

Wait, not like that. I'm just talking about the medications you actually need that the American health care system offers at insane prices. So instead of getting gouged stateside, you pop in to that pharmacy on your trip to Oaxaca and load up on antibiotics and Z-Packs. Perhaps that rash cream that costs you $200 from your doctor in the United States is a measly $15 without a prescription in Mexico. If you are just learning this info, welcome to the good life. But enough of that, let's walk in to my pharmacy. The cocktail pharmacy. We're going to make a smoky penicillin and don't even need a UTI to get it.

1 teaspoon fresh ginger, finely grated
2 ounces mezcal
1½ ounces lemon juice
1 ounce Ginger Simple Syrup (page 229)
Garnish: Slice of dried dragon fruit or
candied ginger (optional)

I like my penicillin with a good spicy kick of ginger, so first I like to finely grate about a teaspoon of fresh ginger into my shaker before moving on to step two. If ginger's not your thing, ignore.

Combine everything except your garnish in a shaker full of ice and go, go, go. Pour over a big rock of ice and garnish with candied ginger. You can totally garnish with a slice of dragon fruit that you dehydrated yourself as pictured here. But, if you are a normal person with other stuff to do, a piece of candied ginger works just fine.

Brûléed Paloma

Makes 1 cocktail

Technically, a paloma is made with grapefruit soda, but sometimes they can be overly sweet. Instead, I like to use fresh grapefruit and add some bubbles with a grapefruit seltzer and a little sweetness with St-Germain. Before you jump down my throat and accuse me of breaking the promise I made not to use a bunch of random liqueurs, let me defend myself!

First, this drink can absolutely use agave or simple syrup instead, and it will be glorious and we can pretend this never happened. However, if you want to grab a tiny bottle of this liqueur, you won't regret it. I get very wary about super floral drinks, but St-Germain is delicate and adds this nice breeze of elderflower beneath what could be a pretty bitter grapefruit drink.

Regardless of your sweet component journey, the real showstopper here is the brûlée garnish. Don't see the word brûlée and get scared. I am not expecting you to go out and buy a tiny torch, or a little gold brûlée gun like mine that I may or may not brandish around the house while pretending to be a Bond girl. This brûlée is actually more of a "broilee," because we only need to use the oven.

1 tablespoon granulated sugar
Slice of grapefruit
2 ounces tequila
2 ounces fresh grapefruit juice
¾ ounce St-Germain (or agave)
Grapefruit seltzer

Let's get our brûlée garnish ready first. Sprinkle the sugar on one side of your grapefruit slice. You want a nice even layer. Then you're simply going to place it on a baking sheet and broil on high for 45 seconds to a minute. You want to pull it once the sugars are bubbling and starting to caramelize, but be careful to take it out before it starts to burn. Once it cools, you're left with a sweet and sour, candy-coated moment to take a bite of between sips.

For the paloma itself, add the tequila, grapefruit juice, and St-Germain to a shaker full of ice and shake till cold. Pour over ice or up then top with a good glug of the seltzer. Garnish!

Corazon Calamari

Serves 4

One 14-ounce can heart of palm
1 egg
½ cup milk
1 cup flour
1 tablespoon Old Bay Seasoning
½ tablespoon garlic powder
Neutral oil for frying

A lot of the recipes in this book are made to look like their meat counterpart so you can surprise your guests when they discover it's actually all veggie. This might be the biggest trickster of them all. I once served this to a friend, and it wasn't until they were halfway through the piping hot basket before they stopped to thank me for generously cooking such a delicious seafood appetizer despite not being able to partake in it. I had that fool fooled!

Serve with Salsa Verde (page 136), or it's also great with the Kickin' Remoulade (page 56).

For the heart of palm, I like to push out any center cores and chop those into 1-inch-long pieces before slicing the rest of the palm into rings.

In one bowl, whisk together the egg and milk. In the other, your flour mixed with the Old Bay and garlic powder. Let your hands play rock-paper-scissors to see who has to be the wet hand, then get in there. Toss your hearts of palm in the egg-and-milk mixture before fully coating it in the flour.

Heat ½ inch to 1 inch of oil in a medium sauté pan over medium–high heat heat. Test one heart of palm to see if the oil is hot enough, then fry in batches until they are crisp, draining the cooked hearts on a paper towel. This process should take only a minute or 2 max for the hearts to crisp up, since nothing needs to be cooked on the inside.

Salsa Verde

Serves 4 to 6

2 pound tomatillos, husked
1 medium onion, peeled and
**   roughly chopped**
2 jalapeños (if you want spicier,
**   go serrano)**
4 garlic cloves
1 tablespoon olive oil
Salt
Pepper
2 limes, juiced
1 cup cilantro

Pico de gallo is the OG. The blueprint for salsa. But my heart belongs to salsa verde. Why? Because I am obsessed with tomatillos. They each come in their own little dress, like they are tiny tomato ballerinas. They are bright and tart. And, although they don't taste exactly the same as tomatoes, they are still incredible when fried up like a green tomato and put on a sandwich with some Oaxacan cheese and—what am I doing? Save it for the second cookbook, Mamrie.

And finally, I love tomatillo salsa because it is so easy. Now, you can totally make this recipe raw by simply throwing all the ingredients (besides the olive oil) in a blender, but we are going a different route. We are just roasting them here because they pair better with tomorrow's MAF. It's so easy that you can make it once and not have to look at the recipe again. So rip this page out! Set it on fire! Fold it into a paper airplane and hit your unsuspecting partner in the head with it.

Preheat the oven to 400°F. Get your tomatillos naked (ha!). This means removing any of the papery outside (the husk) and stem. Tomatillos can be a little sticky so give them a good rinse to get off any residual goo. Chop in quarters and put on a parchment-lined baking sheet along with the onion, jalapeños, and garlic cloves, which you can peel now or after roasting.

Rub everything with the olive oil and give a few good cracks of salt and pepper before placing in the oven, on the top rack, for 10 minutes. After 10, switch from bake to high broil and let them char for 3 to 4 minutes. Take out and cool.

Peel the now-roasted garlic if you haven't already. And cut off the stems of the jalapeños. I like spice, so leave the jalapeño seeds, but now would be the time to remove them if you wanted. Then simply scoop up everything on the pan, including any juices and crusty bits, into a food processor. Add the lime juice and cilantro before pulsing to your ideal texture. Salt and pepper and possibly add back in those jalapeño seeds to taste.

Guava Water

Makes 1 cocktail

1 (nonalcoholic) bottle of
  plain seltzer
2 ounces silver tequila
1 ounce guava nectar
Squeeze of lime

The first time I saw "ranch water" on a menu I was in a fancy chef's restaurant in Texas. Just so we are both clear, "fancy" to me means they have appeared on *Top Chef* at some point, either as a competitor or guest judge.

I ordered it as soon as the server suggested it, and I stopped listening after I heard the word *tequila.* But when it came to me, I was stunned. It was truly just a bottle of Topo Chico with a shot of tequila poured in and garnished with a wedge of lime. What in the upsell was this? That, my friends, is a tequila soda that hired a PR team.

Did I mention I hate tequila and soda? The way I look at it is, if you are drinking good tequila, why dilute it with soda water? And if you are drinking bad tequila, the soda isn't going to mask it. You just have to drink the bad taste for longer. Ranch water to me was just . . . boring. It needed a pop of something unexpected. And that's when I had an idea.

We've all seen the cans of guava juice at the grocery store. Usually in the "international" aisle. A lot of times they are labeled as nectar, and they are amazing. Kind of like if a pear and a strawberry had a love child. Using guava nectar is also a perfect way to energize an otherwise boring combo (bubbly water and tequila) and give your guests a taste they might not have otherwise tried. Plus there are no glasses to wash after!

Open the seltzer and take a couple big swigs out of it. We are making room to then pour in your tequila and guava.

Take a wedge of lime and squeeze it down the bottleneck, then push it in.

Beer-Braised Corona Beans

Serves 4

1 tablespoon butter
1 garlic clove, minced
2 tablespoons oregano, fresh if
  possible, and more for garnish
½ small onion, thinly sliced
1 bell pepper, thinly sliced
1 tablespoon tomato paste
1 pound Royal Corona beans,
  cooked
1½ cups vegetable broth
1½ cups dark Mexican lager
  (like Negra Modelo)
Salt
Pepper
Hot sauce

Despite the title, we are not going to be using Corona beer for the recipe. While I love a cold Corona on a hot summer day as much as Dom Toretto himself, there are more rich and flavorful beers to cook with. But we are going to be using Royal Corona beans!

Royal Corona beans are also known as gigante beans, and for good reason: They are massive. I don't care if that makes me a size queen; I love them. If there is an antipasto bar at a fancy grocery store, I will always grab the cold Greek prepared ones, but here we are serving them piping hot. Don't worry, you can cool your mouth with leftover beer, as we are only using a cup and a half of the bottle here! And if you can't get your hands on Royal Corona beans, pinto beans are a great alternative.

In a medium saucepot, heat the butter before adding the garlic and oregano. Sauté for 1 minute before adding your onions, bell peppers, and tomato paste. Sauté for another 2 to 3 minutes as the veggies sweat and the paste caramelizes.

Add in the beans, broth, and beer and stir. Simmer over low heat for 20 minutes, lid off, to cook out the alcohol and let all the flavors marry. Salt and pepper and hot sauce to taste. Garnish with more fresh oregano.

When it comes to making legumes, bean there, done that. So, let's grab the brew and try something new.

Brussels Sprouts with Lime Crema

Serves 4

For the Brussels Sprouts

1 pound Brussels sprouts, halved
1 tablespoon olive oil
1 tablespoon chili powder
1 tablespoon cumin
1 lime, zested and cut in half
1 cup crema (or Greek yogurt)
1 garlic clove, minced
Salt
Pepper

For the Garnish

**1 cup crumbled cotija cheese or
  queso fresco**
Pickled Fresno Chilies (page 228)

I, too, am shocked and mystified that this is the only Brussels sprouts recipe in this book. But Brussels sprouts have been having such a time on menus these days that it feels like they've all been done. I'm not hating. I love Brussels sprouts. But sometimes they hit the table and they are fried to within an inch of their lives and dry as a bone.

I want creamy Brussels sprouts, not little green tumbleweeds. I think the key to good Brussels sprouts is giving them a hard sear without frizzling, and then complementing them with a creamy element. Because we're going Mexican, crema is the perfect velvety vessel to cool off this chili-spiked brassica.

Preheat the oven to 400°F. Toss the sprouts with the olive oil, chili powder, and cumin. Spread evenly on a parchment-lined pan along with one of the lime halves, cut side down. Pop in the oven for about 20 minutes, or until crispy, flipping halfway through.

For the crema, simply add the lime zest and juice from the other half of the lime into the crema. Mix in the garlic and hit with salt and pepper.

Spread your crema on the plate, then pile the Brussels sprouts on top. Squeeze the roasted lime on top, then garnish with the cheese and chilies.

Cashew Caesar with Spicy Cornflakes

Serves 4

For the Cashew Caesar Dressing

1 cup raw cashews, soaked
   (see steps)
¼ cup olive oil
Juice of one lemon
3 tablespoons grated Parmesan,
   more if needed
2 tablespoons red wine vinegar
1 tablespoon Dijon
1 tablespoon capers,
   more if needed
½ teaspoon Worcestershire
1 garlic clove
Some good cracks of pepper

For the Salad

2 cups plain cornflakes
2 tablespoon butter
1 tablespoon chili powder,
   or less if preferred (or use the
   milder Tajín)
1 tablespoon garlic powder
½ cup grated Parmesan
2 heads radicchio (or whichever
   lettuce you prefer)

Did you know that despite their place on the menu at every checkered tablecloth Italian restaurant in America, Caesar salad was invented in Mexico? That's right. On July 4, 1924, by Caesar Cardini in Tijuana. So, while most Americans set off fireworks and get drunk on boats to honor America's independence, I'm dancing around with a sparkler to pay respect to the greatest salad of all time.

And since I'm not known for being traditional, I'm serving a cashew dressing over gorgeous radicchio and subbing some heat-hittin' cornflake cereal for crunch in place of croutons. If bitter lettuces aren't your thing, this is just as fab with a traditional romaine, kale, or even seared cabbage wedges.

To soak the cashews, place them in a heat-safe bowl or pot (ideally with a lid), boil water, and pour it over the cashews to cover. I let them sit for at least a half hour, but the longer the better (no more than overnight). Then, drain your soaked cashews and put them and all the other dressing ingredients into a food processor or blender and blend until creamy. Taste and see if it needs more capers, Parmesan, and pepper.

For the cornflakes, heat the butter in a small pan before adding the chili powder and garlic powder. These cornflakes are a little spicy, so go milder if you'd prefer less spice. Add in the cornflakes to the melted butter and spices, stirring constantly until they are toasted. Turn off the heat, then stir in the Parmesan.

In a large bowl, toss your radicchio in the dressing or slice lettuce into large chunks and drizzle with dressing. Top with the spicy cornflakes, and I like to add a little shredded Parm. Say a little thank you to the patron saint, Caesar Cardini.

Root al Pastor

Serves 4

For the Marinade

One 1.4-ounce packet of Sazón
   achiote powder
1 big ripe orange
One 14-ounce can pineapple rings
   with no sugar added, in real juice
¼ cup apple cider vinegar
3 to 4 chipotle peppers (canned in
   adobo sauce)
2 tablespoons brown sugar
4 garlic cloves
½ tablespoon ancho chili powder
½ tablespoon ground cumin
½ tablespoon dried oregano

For the Pastor

3 to 4 pounds thick sweet
   potatoes, russets, beets, turnips,
   rutabaga, whatever you like
1 pineapple ring (from can above)
2 tablespoons tomato paste
2 tablespoons honey

As someone who knows how different I look with a five-minute makeup job versus going full glam, I know that good things take time. This looks just like a tiny al pastor you would see under a taco tent in LA, but it is actually layers upon layers of thinly sliced root veggies. It's extra fun to pretend you are a giant crashing someone's taco party. Impress your guests and then serve with tortillas, salsa, and more margaritas.

First, let's make our marinade-sauce combo. Traditional pastor uses an achiote paste, so if you can find it, use it! But as it's harder to come by, I made mine with a Sazón seasoning packet that includes achiote and cilantro. Zest a tablespoon off your orange before adding that and the juice of the whole orange to a blender. Add a cup of the pineapple juice from the canned pineapple and then two pineapple rings. Add all the other marinade ingredients and blend till smooth! Be careful when opening the blender lid because that spice from the marinade will assault your eyes like mace.

If you are using vegetables that need to be peeled, now's the time to do it. I like sweet potato skins but would peel the turnips if you are using those. I also highly recommend a mandolin for super thin, even slices of your root veggies. Once you have a bounty of roots so thin they could be potato chips, place them in a Tupperware or large zip-top bag and pour the marinade into it, making sure every piece is slathered. Stick in the fridge, ideally overnight, or at least a few hours.

After the slices are marinated, preheat the oven to 425°F while you get to stacking them. There are a few ways to do this. You could use a bamboo skewer, and, in that case, I would roast with the widest slices down and then stack up. Or (and this is what is pictured) use a pan that has a kabob stick screwed into it. I got it for like $10 online and love it. Regardless, let's build this beast. It's kind of like a fun puzzle on *Survivor*. Choose your pieces to stack based on diameter, so when finished it resembles an al pastor. Place a chunk of that pineapple ring at the bottom and top of your stack. Save whatever leftover marinade you have left.

Wrap your root pastor lightly in foil, then put in the oven to roast for 90 minutes.

Take a cup of your leftover marinade and add the tomato paste and honey and mix. Now you've got a delicious sauce to slather on the pastor. Once it has roasted for 90 minutes, remove the foil and slather a coating of your marinade sauce. Put back in the oven for 30 minutes before taking out and coating again, and back in for another 30. Keep doing this until the whole shebang is roasted through. Usually around 2.5 hours. You should be left with tender slices and an almost crunchy bark on the outside, like you'd find on BBQ brisket. If you want a little more char, broil that baby.

Take it out, let it cool for a minute, then FEEL cool as you present your masterpiece to your friends. Bust out your sharpest knife and cut long strokes down the edge.

Morning-After Fill: Chilllllaquiles

Serves 2

Leftovers

1 to 2 cups Salsa Verde (page 136)
1 to 2 cups any combo of chopped Root al Pastor (page 145), Brussels Sprouts (page 141), and Beer-Braised Corona Beans (page 139)
Lime Crema (optional; page 141)

Additional Ingredients

One bag of tortilla chips
Eggs
YUP, that's it.
Garnishes, such as Pickled Onions (page 228), Hazelnut Salsa Macha (page 228), or hot sauce

Yes, there are some extra l's in that spelling. That's because we are about to *chilllll* with a big serving of hangover magic. The first time I ever had chilaquiles, I was awestruck. I love nachos, but I always have to ask for extra sauce. I'm a sauce girlie through and through, so when I saw there was a whole other tortilla chip dish that is fully coated in a sauce, my heart sang! No more having to bug the waiter for a seventh tiny ramekin of salsa!

Preheat the oven to 400°F. Open the bag of chips and pour in a cup or two of the leftover salsa verde. Toss in whatever else sounds good. It would be great with more pastor, chopped Brussels sprouts, and, of course, beans. Once you've shaken it all up and the chips are good and coated, dump everything into a baking dish and put it in the oven for 10 to 12 minutes. While that comes together . . .

Cook up eggs how you like them. I like scrambled with mine, so it truly becomes a dish you don't need a knife and fork for. Garnishes: Got pickled onions? Grab 'em. Salsa macha? Let's go. Hot sauce. Lime crema. Take out your chilaquiles from the oven, top with the eggs, and whatever else you want.

THE UNDERDOGS

It's high time these
overlooked fruits and vegetables get
their moment in the spotlight.

This chapter is about the weirdos of the produce world. The ones that haven't had their leading role. The ones that aren't basking in the warmth of accolades from fine dining chefs and hot spots with New American menus. The ones that are harnessing so much potential and flavor but always get overlooked.

Consider them like Rachael Leigh Cook in *She's All That*. The girl only needed to ditch the glasses and the overalls for people to realize a hot babe was simmering underneath. That's how I feel about these fruits and veggies. So, cue up "Kiss Me" by Sixpence None the Richer because these ingredients are about to walk down the stairs.

RECIPES

Apricot Sour

Makes 1 cocktail

1 tablespoon apricot jam
2 ounces whiskey
1 ounce lemon juice
Lemon, cherry, or dried apricot
for garnish

Don't worry. I'm not going to have you source fresh apricots to make this drink. Instead, we'll be using a thinned-out fruit jam. It's an excellent shortcut to making perfect drinks in a jiffy. Pro tip: A great way to use the last little bit of jam in a jar is to make a cocktail in the jar, and then use it as a shaker. I'm making this drink with whiskey, but it would be excellent with bourbon, tequila, gin, vodka, or rum!

In an empty shaker, add the jam and whiskey, either stirring or shaken until they've come together. I do this before adding ice so the jam melts into the liquor rather than seizing up and remaining a glob when it gets cold. We are going for low viscosity here.

Add the lemon juice and ice and shake till cold, straining over a big ice cube or served in a coupe. Garnish with lemon, a cherry, or a dried apricot.

It's about time we appreciate the apricot.

Fennel Fizz

Makes 1 cocktail

Fennel?! In a drink?! Yes. I am doing it and you can't stop me. There's something about the almost-licorice flavor of raw fennel that when mixed with the bitterness of tonic just works. It's really anise combo. They could be best fronds.

   I'll only agree to stop doing puns if you give this drink a chance! And that is my fennel offer.

1 tablespoon chopped fennel or a few slices, plus a frond for garnish
2 ounces good gin
¾ ounce lime juice
2 dashes Angostura bitters
Tonic to top

In an empty shaker, muddle your fennel. Once you are getting wafts of licorice, add the gin, lime juice, and ice and shake it all up.

Strain into your glass with ice, add the bitters, then top with the tonic. Garnish with the most obnoxious frond you can find.

Belle of the Ball Margarita

Makes 1 cocktail

We've all seen peppers in a margarita, which give it some spice. But what about a pepper that makes it nice? If you want to serve someone a drink that is drop-dead gorgeous and has a certain je ne sais quoi, this is your drink. You start by juicing red bell peppers. Stay with me. I know it's out of the box. But the red bell pepper creates this sweet, vegetal, and bright red juice that pairs perfectly with the citrus in a margarita.

2 ounces red bell pepper juice (see Sidenote)
2 ounces good tequila
1 ounce lime juice
1 ounce orange liqueur
Salt for rim (optional)

You know the drill. Combine everything except the salt in a shaker full of ice, then strain into a cute up glass or glass with fresh ice. Would be delicious with a spicy salt rim.

Sidenote
Ideally, you will run your bell peppers through a juicer. But if you don't have a juicer, you can always put the red bell peppers in a blender with a little water, blend till smooth, and then run the mixture through a mesh strainer or coffee filter. Either way, you typically need one bell pepper per drink.

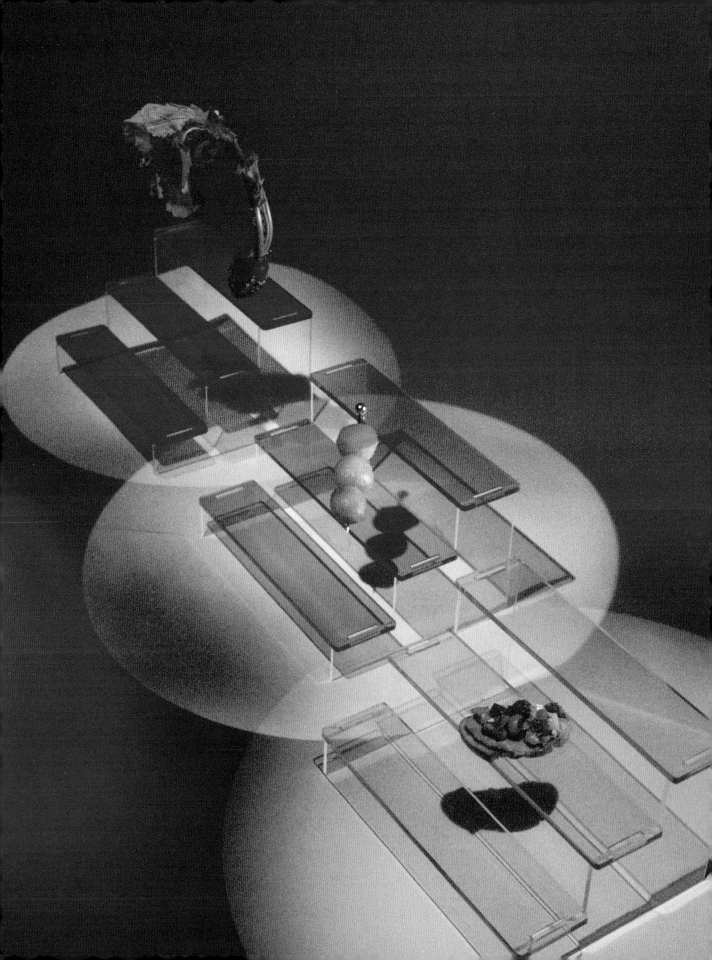

Trio of Canapes

Savory Pickled Cantaloupe

Serves 4 to 6

**Either 8 slices of cantaloupe or
 24 small balls**
**2 cups white or champagne
 vinegar**
1 cup water
½ cup sugar
1 tablespoon salt
**1 teaspoon whole black
 peppercorns**
1 teaspoon cloves
1 cinnamon stick, broken in half
3 star anise pods

It's time to put some respect on cantaloupes. They have come a long way since the '80s when people would just slice them in half and stuff them with cottage cheese. Be honest, you probably only eat cantaloupe when you go to brunch and somehow resist potatoes and order a side of fruit instead. And they're not even top-billing there. They are simply filler at the bottom of the bowl, holding up the coveted berries that rest on top.

But we are celebrating cantaloupe here by carving them into perfect spheres (slices work too). Then we . . . get this . . . pickle them! But not just with a random dill combo. We are going savory with cloves, cinnamon, and star anise. It's a surprising bite that finally treats cantaloupe right.

Heat everything but the cantaloupe in a pot over high heat. Once it comes to a boil, reduce to a simmer and let it go for another 5 minutes. You don't want it to reduce, per se, but you want all those aromatics to release their fragrant oils. Then take off the heat and let cool completely. While that is happening . . .

In a Tupperware, place your melon-balled cantaloupe or lay down your slices. Once the pickling liquid is cool, pour over the cantaloupe and seal tight. Let it marinate for at least an hour but no more than 12 to retain the fresh texture of the melon.

These Radishes Are Everything

Serves 4

1 stick (½ cup) unsalted butter
Dozen or so breakfast radishes
  (or regular but the more petite
  the better)
4 tablespoons everything bagel
  seasoning

The only other time we've used radish in this book was for the I'm All Ears Pasta Salad (page 48), and that was as a garnish. Too often, radishes are taken advantage of for their crunch. People cast them to the side as background talent that just adds a little texture to someone else's starring role. Well, no more! Radishes can stand on their own.

Especially when dipped in butter and sprinkled with garlic, poppy, sesame, onion, and salt. What you're left with is one rad . . . dish.

(I'm sorry.)

In a double boiler (a heat-resistant bowl on top of a pot of boiling water), melt the stick of butter halfway before bringing off the heat. You can also just do this in a microwave and keep an eye on it in 30-second intervals. Use a whisk or fork to melt the rest of the butter until it's all smooth and opaque. You don't want just yellow melted butter like for popcorn. This version is tempered.

Make sure you have a pan or counter lined with parchment paper before you start dipping. Then one by one dip the radishes two-thirds of the way into the tempered butter. Lay them to cool on the parchment and sprinkle with the seasoning while they are still hot.

Lie to your drunkest guest by saying it's a chocolate-dipped strawberry and record their reaction.

Black-Eyed Pea Cowboy Crostini

Serves 4 to 6

For the Hummus

One 16-ounce bag of frozen
   black-eyed peas (canned
   works too)
3 tablespoons tahini, more if
   needed
Juice of one lemon
2 tablespoons olive oil
3 garlic cloves
1 tablespoon smoked paprika
½ tablespoon ground cumin
Salt
Pepper

For the Cowboy Caviar

One 16-ounce bag of frozen
   black-eyed peas
½ cup feta cheese
½ cup corn kernels
½ cup diced tomatoes
½ cup chopped cilantro
½ onion, diced
¼ cup diced pickled jalapeños
2 tablespoons red wine or apple
   cider vinegar
1 tablespoon lime juice
1 garlic clove, diced
Salt to taste
Pepper to taste

Crostini slices or crackers

Black-eyed peas never reached the popularity that they deserve. Part of me thinks it's because of the pop group of the 2000s of the same name. If you tell a millennial that you are making black-eyed peas for dinner, you are essentially cursing them, because they will have "Let's Get It Started" in their head all night. God forbid, they will also start picturing Fergie doing those cartwheels on the *Today Show.*

Or perhaps they are underappreciated because they got the short stick when it comes to names. Snap peas sound like a legume I would want to go dancing with. Snow peas for sure own a time-share in Vail. Chickpeas sound like they'd ignore you at a party. But poor black-eyed peas make me want to call protective services.

Today we are putting paprika-pinched black-eyed pea hummus atop a crunchy crostini, because everything is fancier when atop a tiny toast. But, not only that, we are also topping it with a classic cowboy caviar that stays put thanks to the creamy dip below it.

More than likely, but double-check, your frozen black-eyed peas were flash-steamed before frozen. So all you will need to do is blanch both bags of them. If you are using canned, be sure to thoroughly rinse off the aquafaba. Pat dry and let cool. It is a *lot* of black-eyed peas, but we are using them two ways. Set aside a cup for tomorrow's MAF.

Take half of the remaining peas and add to a food processor with the tahini, lemon, olive oil, garlic, paprika, cumin, and salt and pepper to taste. Blend until smooth. If it's too thick, add a splash of water. Too thin, pop in some more tahini.

Combine the cowboy caviar ingredients and toss. If you have time to let it marinate for an hour, awesome. Spread your hummus on your crostini and top with the caviar. Or go the dip route and serve with some crackers. Yeehaw!

Ants on a Log Celery Salad

Serves 4

3 large celery ribs
1 green apple
2 to 3 cups arugula
1 cup raisins
1 cup Peanut Sauce (page 229)

Celery is way more talented than we give it credit for. Think about how many things it's in, serving as a backbone of flavor and depth without ever stepping into the spotlight. It's like the bassist of the vegetable world. A member of both the French pop group, Mirepoix, and the Cajun jazz band, the Holy Trinity.

I, too, have taken celery's culinary importance for granted. As I get older, I try to incorporate celery into a lot more of my cooking but, for this dish, I wanted to take it back to the first time I ever liked it to begin with. Kindergarten. Back when it would be smothered in peanut butter and dotted with raisins. I was never sold on this herbal veggie back then, but you got to pretend you were eating ants, so my weird kid self was stoked! Here's the grown-up version of the snack time classic.

Totally optional, but I like to soak my raisins in boiling water for 5 minutes or so, to rehydrate and plump them up. Next, time to chop. I keep the celery chunky and just cut it on a bias for more of a rustic, deli-style salad, but feel free to mandolin it thinly or however you prefer. For the apples, I cut them into matchstick shapes.

Toss all the ingredients together, saving a few raisins to look like they are ants crawling down to the plate. This is not optional. This is a mandatory step.

Parsnips with Hazelnut Macha

Serves 4

1 pound parsnips
2 tablespoons olive oil
1½ teaspoons garlic powder
Salt
Pepper
Hazelnut Salsa Macha (page 228)
Lemon wedge
Pinch of Parsley

Walking through the produce aisle, it's easy to see why someone would reach for a carrot instead of a parsnip. Sure, they're sisters. They resemble each other greatly. But side by side, parsnips look like the pale, goth, big-boned sibling beside the tan and slender one. The bigger sister is sent to chaperone the younger one's date and act as a possible bodyguard.

But when you get to know this root, you will see that she is not only sweeter but way more interesting. No offense to carrots. Whom I adore. But parsnips will surprise you. They've got notes of cinnamon and nutmeg. A light backbone of licorice. And when paired with the acidic, spicy uppercut that is Hazelnut Salsa Macha, well, consider this the third act of the musical *Gypsy*, 'cause this sister is ready to take the stage!

Cooking parsnips couldn't be easier. Wash 'em good. I never peel my parsnips because I think they have natural beauty and don't need to conform to the peeled expectations society places on them, but that's me. Slice in half lengthwise. Toss in the olive oil and garlic powder and give it a crack of salt and pepper, before spreading across a baking sheet.

Put in a 400°F oven for 20 minutes, giving a toss halfway through. As that roasts, make the Hazelnut Salsa Macha (page 228).

They should come out nice and roasted with a little caramelization. Plate them up and give a good smear of salsa macha, a squeeze of lemon, and parsley.

Give carrots the 'snip.

Sunday Celery Root

Serves 4

For the Celery Root
2 large celery roots
2 cups dill pickle juice
1 cup sour cream or
** unflavored yogurt**
2 eggs
2 to 3 cups oil (peanut
** or vegetable)**
Dipping sauce (I like the Kickin'
** Remoulade, page 56)**

For the Breading Mix
1½ cups all-purpose flour
1½ tablespoons powdered sugar
1 tablespoon garlic powder
1½ teaspoons paprika
1 teaspoon celery salt
1 teaspoon salt
1 teaspoon pepper
½ teaspoon baking powder

Let's talk celery root. The lesser celebrated half of the celery. I know the stalks are also in this chapter, but the root gets even less respect! Hiding out underground, searching for all the nutrients, while its flashier green counterpart is just sitting out in the sun. Eventually, to be snatched up and plunged into a cold pool of tomato juice and vodka.

But we can't neglect the root, because it is delicious! For a long time, I didn't think anything of it. I'd see it at the grocery store and think "Celeriac? Isn't that when someone has a gluten allergy?" and then I keep moseying down the produce aisle. Celery root has never really caught on in the States. That changes today. It's sweet, nutty, and crunchy with a little backbone of celery flavor. And when you cook it, it gets more fibrous, making it a great meat substitute.

The "Sunday" in the recipe name is in honor of a couple of ingredients. You might be familiar with a certain popular chicken fast-food chain that isn't open on the Lord's Day. The internet is torn on exactly what their secrets are, but I've taken several cues and found the best version for me. Spoiler: It's the pickle juice brine, a little powdered sugar in the breading, and frying in peanut oil. Plus a few of my own tweaks. It will give the celery root all the (Fil-a) flavor with none of the homophobia.

Peel the celery roots and cut into chunks like potato wedges. They can also be sliced more like a fillet, but I'm going for handheld and dippable. Once the roots are all cut up, place them in a zip-top bag or sealable container. Mix the pickle juice with the sour cream and coat the root in it. Make sure all the chunks are covered, then let marinate overnight or at least an hour or 2.

Once you're ready to fry, set up the batter station. Whisk the eggs in a bowl. In another bowl, sift together all the breading ingredients. This is the only time you should ever double dip. That's right. One by one, coat the celery root chunks in the egg, then the breading mix, back to the egg, and then the breading mix until they are all coated.

Heat the oil. The fast-food chain uses peanut oil but vegetable works just as well. Then, without overcrowding the pan, fry them up, for 2 to 3 minutes on each side till golden brown before draining any excess oil on a paper towel. Serve with your favorite dipping sauce.

Morning-After Fill: Kitchen Sink Sliders

Serves 4

Leftovers

2 cups leftover Parsnips with Hazelnut Macha (page 160) and/or Sunday Celery Root (de-breaded; page 163)
½ cup Cowboy Caviar (page 157)
3 tablespoons Black-Eyed Pea Hummus (page 157), more if needed

Extra Ingredients

Pack of Hawaiian rolls
1 cup quick-cooking oats, more if needed
1 egg
Oil for the pan
1 cup of your favorite BBQ sauce
Feta for topping (optional)

Why make one burger when you could make half a dozen little guys and lord over a tiny burger audience? Go full Jughead from the Archie comics and make a pyramid of them. Dislocate that jaw and stack them there deep. There is no wrong way to eat a tiny burger. It's only wrong to not eat it at all.

This recipe is a roadmap. I suggest some fillings and toppings, but you can use this general recipe with leftovers from tons of meals. Go where your tastebuds take you, because your butt will be taking you to that couch to veg out.

In a food processor, add a cup or so of leftover parsnip and/or celery root with the breading taken off. Give it a couple of whirls to dice up. (We add the root veg first so we don't end up with just a paste.) Then add the hummus, Cowboy Caviar, oats, and egg. Give this another few pulses.

The mixture should hold together to form patties. If it's too wet, add some more oats. Too dry? Add another big dollop of hummus. Form into small patties and fry like you would a burger in a skillet with a little oil for about 2 minutes on each side. I like to slather on a BBQ sauce and top with feta before hitting them with a minute of broil.

Build those sliders and possibly a fort in the living room.

Ya'll, let's whip up some super-fast sliders and slide our asses onto the couch!

LET'S FRENCH!

Have *merci*! These dishes from France will make you want to dance. Worried you can't cook French food? Yes, you cancan!

Julia Child once said, "In France, cooking is a serious art form and a national sport." Fantastic! I've never been a sports fan anyway. The only reason I'm watching the Super Bowl is to peruse the snack table. And every three years or so I go to a Dodgers game specifically for a veggie dog and beer combo.

But cooking as a sport? Hell, yeah! I would gladly rock a jersey with my favorite foods embroidered between the shoulders instead of the name of a player. I'd buy trading cards with chef's stats. Now that I think about it, I could really go for a Chicago Bears hat but the logo says Beers. Green Bay Packers? Gimme them Snackers. The Seattle Marinaras. The New York Knishs. The Baltimore Oreos.

Back to Julia. She was right. The French do not mess around when it comes to cooking. Their recipes are precise. And technically advanced. And we are going to bastardize the hell out of them. We do not have time to attend Le Cordon Bleu. Fingers crossed that people don't say we Cordon Bleu it . . .

RECIPES

Lavender Lemon Drop

LET'S FRENCH!

Makes 1 cocktail

**1 tablespoon or 1 tea bag butterfly
pea flower tea (optional)**
2½ ounces vodka
1½ ounces lemon juice
**1 ounce lavender simple syrup
(see steps for instructions)**
Lavender sugar rim or plain sugar

I am obsessed with lemon drop martinis. To me, they are the perfect drink. For this French twist on it, I pictured sipping on a tart lemon drop martini in the South of France while standing in a field of lavender, the breeze catching the soft powdery aroma and lightly kissing the top of my drink to give it a subtle tinge of floral.

That got romantic quick! If this whole cookbook thing doesn't work out, I think I have romance novelist as a possible fall-back career.

Out of the gate, I must tell you how I got this gorgeous color you see on the page before you. That is from a little thing called a butterfly pea flower. All I did was soak a tablespoon (or a tea bag) in my vodka for an hour before making the drink to get a gorgeous blue hue. One bag will be enough to get this color for 8 ounces or so. Then when you add lemon juice to it, it turns purple. But it has zero effect on the taste, so if you don't do this step you, you will still end up with a Lavender Lemon Drop that is the classic pale yellow.

For the lavender simple syrup, either use fresh lavender or dried buds if you can get your mitts on them. If not just find a lavender tea. Even in the most country of grocery stores, you will be able to find a lavender with chamomile. Make your simple syrup on the stovetop as usual (1 cup water, 1 cup sugar) but add 2 to 3 tea bags or 2 tablespoons of the fresh or dried buds. After it reaches a boil, turn off the heat and let the bags steep in the syrup while it cools. This should make enough for 8 drinks. But you can totally store it in an airtight jar in the fridge, and it's lovely in a hot tea or as sweetener in a lavender latte the next morning!

Combine all the ingredients in a shaker full of ice and shake until your hands are cold. Pour into a cutie pie coupe rimmed with sugar. For a little extra pump of lavender, grind a tablespoon of lavender buds or empty a dry lavender tea bag and mix with the sugar.

Bloody Mary Butter

Serves 4

1 stick (½ cup) unsalted, room-temp butter
2 tablespoons tomato paste
1 tablespoon sun-dried tomatoes, finely chopped
1 tablespoon grated horseradish
½ teaspoon celery seed
1 garlic clove, minced or finely grated
½ teaspoon Worcestershire

Little known fact, the Bloody Mary was invented in Paris in 1920. A well-known fact, I freaking love Bloody Marys. I once threw an event called the Bloody Mary'thon where I organized 50-plus people, dressed in '80s workout gear, to do a full Bloody Mary bar crawl alongside the actual New York City Marathon. This was complete with one of those run-by water stations, but with Dixie cups filled with mimosas instead!

I've only done it once, but the heartburn will live forever. Here, we are taking the flavors of a Bloody Mary and infusing them into an adorable tomato-shaped butter.

Simply mix everything together in either a food processor or just use a fork and make sure to get everything super incorporated. That's it.

Put your now-infused butter in the fridge till it's workable like Play-Doh. Roll into one large or several small tomato shapes. Pop on a real tomato stem to really nail the presentation.

We are turning this cocktail on its head . . . and spreading it on bread.

Truffle Shuffle Butter

Serves 4

1 stick (½ cup) unsalted butter
½ teaspoon of either truffle oil or
    truffle pâté
1 tablespoon grated Parmesan
½ tablespoon garlic powder
Salt
Lots of cracked pepper to taste
1 tablespoon unsweetened cocoa

I call this butter the Truffle Shuffle, not because of my love of *The Goonies*, which is real and burns bright. It's because it is another recipe that tricks the diner. We are pretty much just making a truffle compound butter but shaping it to look like a real truffle, giving it a dusting of cocoa powder as if it was just pulled out of the dirt, and serving it frozen so that it can be shaved tableside.

Of course, this over-the-top presentation is optional. If you are worried the butter will be too cold, don't be. It is shaved so thin that by the time you hit it with your butter knife it spreads nice and smooth.

Get the butter to room temp before mixing in your truffle oil, Parmesan, garlic powder, salt, and pepper. Whip it all together before molding it into truffle shapes. Maybe you have just one big one. Perhaps individual small ones so each guest gets their own! However, you like. If the butter gets too soft to mold, just stick it in the freezer for 5 to 10 minutes. Final step: using a paper towel as a brush, brush the lightest coating of unsweetened cocoa powder on the butter. Make it look like it was just pulled out of the dirt. This will absolutely make your hands dirty if you end up shaving the butter, but it's worth it for the realism.

Citrus Sidepiece

Makes 1 cocktail

2 ounces cognac
¾ ounce orange liqueur
½ ounce lemon juice
½ ounce blood orange juice

This is a play on the classic sidecar cocktail. Instead of using just lemon as the citrus element, I also add some freshly squeezed blood orange juice. Then I garnish it, not only with a little sliver of blood orange, but also a tiny second Sidepiece! Like the little sidecar on a motorcycle, it's there for you to top off your drink when it gets a little too low for your liking.

Combine everything in a shaker with ice. Shake until cold, then serve either in a glass over a single, big ice cube or up. A traditional sidecar has a sugar rim but I prefer without. You do you!

Cognac is my favorite brandy.
"Brandy" is my favorite yacht rock song.

Camembert and Berry Brûlée

Serves 4

1 cup of your favorite berries (I like blackberries)
4 tablespoons cognac
8-ounce wheel of Camembert cheese
½ tablespoon granulated sugar
Baguette

What's better than cheese? Cheese with booze in it, baby! Not to mention the sweet and acidic tang of your favorite berry. This recipe can be done with Brie but Camembert is a little bolder. Aged less than Brie, Camembert still has its wild child ways.

This couldn't be easier. Toss the berries in the cognac. Cut the Camembert into 1-inch chunks or triangles. Then arrange them in an oven-safe dish, pouring any excess cognac over the top. Bake at 350°F for 15 to 20 minutes until ooey-gooey.

At the last minute, sprinkle the sugar on top and hit it with a broil for a little brûlée. Serve with a baguette.

No rind left behind. It's perfectly fine to eat!

Nice'oise Salad

Serves 4

For the Chickpea Tuna Dip

1 garlic clove
2 celery stalks, roughly chopped
2 green onions
Two 16-ounce cans chickpeas,
drained and rinsed
¼ cup tahini or sour cream
Juice of half a lemon
1 tablespoon Dijon mustard
2 tablespoon capers, chopped
1 tablespoon seafood seasoning
(like Old Bay)
Lots of cracked black pepper
Salt
¼ cup chopped fresh dill

Salad Suggestions

Handful of blanched green beans
Thinly sliced cucumber
Diced olives
Jammy eggs
Halved cherry tomatoes
2 cups potato chips (I do this
for crunch instead of boiled
potatoes)

For the Sherry
Shallot Vinaigrette

1 small shallot, minced
1 clove garlic, minced
½ cup sherry or white wine
vinegar
¼ cup olive oil
1 tablespoon Dijon
Salt to taste
Pepper to taste

As someone who loves to build a perfect bite, sometimes Niçoise salads are just the ticket. But I'd never order one at a restaurant because I don't want to say, "Hold the tuna" but also "Can you make it like eight bucks cheaper because I didn't get the fish?" It would be a rip-off order. Today, we are putting the nice in Niçoise by skipping the fish and using chickpeas instead, with capers and seafood seasoning to get that briny ocean vibe. It's part salad, part dip, all delicious.

Put the garlic, celery, and green onions in a food processor and give a few pulses to chop before adding in the rest of the chickpea tuna ingredients, except for the dill. Blend until smooth, or the consistency you prefer. I still like a little chunkiness. Fold in the dill, then start on the salad portion.

Whisk the vinaigrette ingredients in large bowl before tossing your preferred salad ingredients (except potato chips) in the dressing. Spread some of the chickpea dip on half of your plate then pile the dressed salad up beside it. Garnish with a stack of crunchy potato chips or crunch them in your hands and sprinkle on top.

Carrot Ribbons à l'Orange

Serves 4

4 to 5 carrots
1 stick (½ cup) butter (it's French, after all)
½ cup shallots, minced
1 tablespoon five-spice powder
1 tablespoon orange zest
¼ cup orange juice
2 tablespoons orange liqueur
2 tablespoons red wine vinegar
Salt
Pepper
Tarragon or chervil to garnish

The first time I went to Paris with my fiancé, I asked everyone for food recs. My friend Val insisted we had to go to Café Les Deux Magots for the duck à l'orange. So we tucked into a tiny two-top, wedged between old French men swilling Chablis at noon and having a heated conversation about who knows what. And I watched my guy swoon over their signature dish. He couldn't believe it. Sure, my soup was great but watching him have a transcendental experience filled me with jealousy. He still talks about it. If he saw a duck in a pond right now, he'd go, "What was that place we went to in Paris?"

Despite not being able to partake in that food euphoria, I absolutely did dip some bread in the orange glaze, and I knew why this place was famous. I'd been chasing the dragon ever since. And then one day I decided try my hand at combining these flavors with something I knew would pair well. Carrots. But since we are in Paris mode and want it to be heavy on the whimsy, we are not only shaving the carrots into ribbons so you can twirl them on your fork like a pasta, but we are cooking them *en papillote*. In paper. It's like opening up a little individually wrapped present for your palate.

Preheat the oven to 375°F. Using a vegetable peeler, cut the carrots into ribbons. I think one big carrot per person works. Set out four pieces of parchment, about a square foot each. Portion out the carrots evenly on each, placing them in the center.

In a small saucepot, melt the butter, then add the shallots and five-spice powder. Stir for a minute before adding the orange zest, juice, liqueur, and vinegar. I add a few good cracks of salt and pepper. Let that simmer over low heat for 3 to 5 minutes before taking off the heat to cool.

Spoon the sauce over the carrots evenly, giving them a toss before sealing up your parchment. Bake for 15 to 20 minutes before unwrapping and garnishing with tarragon.

Serves 4

1-pound bag of frozen pearl
   onions, thawed
2 tablespoons unsalted butter,
   more if needed
2 garlic cloves, chopped
1 tablespoon cognac
1 tablespoon balsamic vinegar
½ cup white wine
½ cup veggie stock
1½ teaspoons not-beef bouillon
1 tablespoon fresh thyme leaves
2 cups grated Gruyère
1 cup bread crumbs or crushed
   butter crackers

French onion soup is iconic. Stuffing a whole grilled cheese's worth of bread and Gruyère into a bowl and pretending like it's a light start is my kind of delusion. For my take on the classic, I am ditching the broth and getting right to the good stuff. Delicate pearl onions are concentrated with the French onion flavor and baked with tons of Gruyère and breadcrumbs to turn this soup into a hearty casserole-style side dish.

Frozen veggies are magic but sometimes they have a lot of extra water in there. So make sure you start with thawed, room-temp onions, Drain any excess water and use paper towels to squeeze them to get out any more hiding in there. In a medium saucepan, melt the butter over medium–low heat. Add the onions. Slowly cook them, stirring frequently. We are going for caramelized, so make sure the butter doesn't burn and add a little more if you need. This should take 12 to 15 minutes.

Once you have a good brown color, add the garlic, cognac, and balsamic. The cognac will deglaze the pan and should help scrape up any bits off the bottom. Cook over low heat for another 1 minute before adding the white wine, veggie stock, not-beef bouillon, and thyme. Simmer for another 5 minutes on low, reducing the liquid in half.

Put the onions in a baking dish or leave them in the skillet if it's oven-safe. Make sure they are nice and even before topping with your Gruyère and bread crumbs and broiling on low until the top is ooey-gooey like a bowl of the soup it's in honor of.

Lemony Bow Ties with Spinach and Asparagus

Serves 4

**One 16-ounce box farfalle
  or mini farfalle
Salt
2 tablespoons olive oil
2 cups chopped asparagus
2 tablespoons butter
2 garlic cloves, minced
1 cup dry white wine
2 tablespoons lemon juice
1 tablespoon lemon zest
1 cup heavy cream
Pepper
½ cup Parmesan, finley grated,
  more if needed
2 cups baby spinach**

This dish has more bow ties than the waitstaff at the Moulin Rouge. Here, we are making a creamy, decadent pasta with all the trappings of a French bistro. And by that I mean a ton of cream, butter, and cheese.

Absolutely use store-bought pasta to make your life easier. I sure did. But, if you're wondering why one of the bow ties in the accompanying photo is on steroids, it's because I rolled out a sheet of pasta to create this mother bow tie. This is not in any way necessary, but it will make your guests ooh and aah.

Get a big pot of water boiling for your pasta. Be sure to salt it! Cook as directed, and while that boils . . .

Heat the olive oil in a large saucepan, then give your asparagus a sauté for 2 to 3 minutes. Take out your asparagus and set it to the side.

Using the same saucepan, add the butter and garlic. Let the garlic sweat for a minute or 2 before adding the white wine. Then let that cook off for another 2 to 3 minutes to reduce the alcohol before adding in your lemon juice, zest, and heavy cream. Your sauce should be starting to come together. I like to give it a few big cracks of pepper before folding in the Parmesan.

Add in your pasta, sautéed asparagus, and then your spinach. Those spinach leaves will cook down, truly, in 30 seconds. Plate it up, add more Parmesan. Hide it under a giant homemade bow tie because you live for the drama!

You will farfalle in love with this dish.

The False Financier

Makes 1 cocktail

For the Almond Simple Syrup
1 cup water
1 cup sugar
1 teaspoon almond extract

For the Cocktail
2½ ounces Vanilla Bean Vodka (page 83)
¾ ounce amaretto
½ ounce Almond Simple Syrup
Squeeze of lemon

For the "Olives"
Marzipan
Green food coloring
Yellow food coloring

What you might see before you looks like a perfectly dirty, cold martini. But, nay! This drink is not what it seems. Those are not olives. Those are marzipan. That isn't a briny libation. It's an almond affair! What you've got here are all the flavors of a financier cookie you would find at a local patisserie pretending to be the star of a martini bar.

First, make your simple syrup, which is simple as can be. You're making it like every other simple, heating the water in a small saucepan and adding the sugar and stirring until dissolved. The only difference is you are going to add the extract to it as well. Wait for it to cool to use in drinks; it can be stored in an airtight container for up to 2 weeks; and be sure to add to your iced coffee tomorrow.

Time to form our garnish: To get this brilliant green with the marzipan, I added 2 parts blue to 1 part yellow food coloring, as opposed to just using a green food coloring. Knead the food coloring into the marzipan until it's the correct olive shade that you want. I form them into olive shapes, then I use a straw to poke out the inside so they are pitted. Keep cool in the fridge while you make the drink.

Put all the cocktail ingredients in a shaker full of ice, make it as cold as you can, then pour into a frosted martini glass. Garnish with your sweet olives!

Morning-After Fill: Cremeux Pot Pie

Serves 2

Leftovers

3 cups of any combo of Carrot Ribbons à l'Orange (page 178), Like One of Your French Pearls (page 181), and celery and blanched green beans from Nice'oise Salad (page 177)

New Ingredients

3 tablespoons butter
1 tablespoon poultry seasoning
1 cup frozen hashbrowns (the shredded kind)
¼ cup flour
1 cup veggie stock
1 cup white wine
Splash of heavy cream
Salt
Pepper
Thawed puff pastry or pie crust
1 egg

Few things give me as much joy as having people over for dinner and getting to say "Oh, that? Yeah, I made it from scratch." That said, sometimes the only scratch I have is scratching my head wondering why I didn't save time and go store-bought.

One of them is puff pastry. It takes forever! Have you ever watched a season of *The Great British Bake Off*?! Watch it. The first thing you will think is, *Good lord, Noel Fielding is charming. Do you think he's only attracted to fellow goths or do you think I have a shot?* But the NEXT thing you will think is, *I can't believe how laborious it is to make a croissant-like dough.* I do not have the patience nor do I have the wrist strength to be rolling dough all day. Enter . . . puff pastry.

Store-bought puff pastry is magic, and is the hero one needs to make the easiest pot pie out there. It's all the buttery comfort with way less risk of carpal tunnel.

Preheat the oven to 375°F. First, let's wrangle up the veggies for the filling. If you have leftover carrot ribbons, give them a rinse and pat them dry to get off any remaining orange vinaigrette. I love five-spice, but not in this pot pie. Give them a quick chop and add a cup or so to a cup of leftover pearl onions, and a cup of the leftover blanched green beans from the Nice'oise Salad (page 177). Since I didn't make boiled baby potatoes for the salad and used potato chips instead, this is where the frozen hashbrowns come in.

Choose a saucepan or deep cast iron that you will bake in. You can always transfer the mixture to a baking dish but I'm trying to save you from dirty dishes here. In that pan, melt your butter over medium heat. Add the poultry seasoning. If you have a cup of leftover diced celery, add that too and let it sweat for a minute.

Now sprinkle in the flour and stir with the melted butter so that it forms an almost paste-like consistency. Let that brown for a moment before slowly pouring in your veggie stock and white wine. Don't rush this! Add the liquid little by little and use a whisk if you have one.

Keep stirring and this will make a gravy sort of consistency. Toss in your leftover veggies and shredded hashbrowns. Let all this bubble and cook and thicken for a few minutes before adding in a splash of cream. Taste for salt and pepper. Once it's reached that ideal pot-pie thickness, take off the heat and let it cool enough to be able to touch the edge of the pan. Roll out the puff pastry. Place the puff pastry over the top of the veggies, pinching the sides to secure it to the pan. Whisk your egg with a splash of water, then brush over the top. Cut a few little slits for steam to escape before placing it in the oven till the top is golden and crispy (according to the puff or crust baking instructions).

Draw the curtains. Put on the guilty pleasure TV show. There is zero shame in eating straight out of the pan with a towel across your lap.

THE SPICE IS RIGHT

The food will have your
tongue tingling, and the drinks
will have your guests mingling.

Don't fret. Not everything you make from the recipes in this chapter will be spicy. Although they absolutely can be if you set your mind to it. All these dishes are, however, packed to the thrills with flavor. That's because they use some of my favorite ingredients from Southeast Asia as well as from Korea and, fine, cream cheese from America.

What I'm saying is these are my favorite ways of cooking with Asian ingredients at home in my style. These are in no way traditional, because I will never be able to make those foods of these cultures like the folks who have been mastering them forever. What I'm trying to say is . . . I'm a white girl from North Carolina. I am not going to try and make traditional cuisine here, y'all.

RECIPES

Roasted Mango Salsa with Rice Paper Flowers

Serves 4

For the Salsa
3 cups ripe mango chunks
   (fresh or thawed frozen)
1 cup red onion, chopped
1 red bell pepper, chopped
2 tomatoes, halved
2 Fresno or habanero chilies,
   halved (see Sidenote)
2 garlic cloves
2 tablespoons olive oil
Juice of 2 limes
1 cup cilantro
Salt
Pepper

For the Rice Paper Flowers
Rice paper
Precooked rice (jasmine, coconut,
   whichever you've got)
Tablespoon of turmeric
Vegetable or peanut oil

I know that salsa is not an Asian dish, but mango? Cilantro? Lime? We love a culture-crossing ingredients list. This salsa is delicious when prepared raw, but we are going to roast our ingredients to give them that much more depth. She is sweet. She is spicy. She is served along some adorable fried rice paper flowers because even salsa can be an event.

This couldn't be easier. If you made the Salsa Verde (page 136), this recipe is the same method. Simply put everything from the salsa list—except the lime, cilantro, salt, and pepper—on a sheet pan and toss in the olive oil. Stick in a 400°F oven and bake for 15 minutes. Turn the oven to broil and add a minute of broiling at the end if you want that charred, smoky flavor.

Blend the roasted ingredients along with the cilantro and lime juice. Salt and pepper to taste. While that cools . . .

Cut the rice paper into flowers. I just cut into the paper to make petals but still keep the original size of the paper. If you want a double-layer flower like the ones pictured, simply take a teaspoon of cooked rice to use as a glue in between 2 flowers. The stamen is another piece of rice colored with turmeric. I use store-bought rice or use a few teaspoons of Coconut Rice (page 193) and swirl my turmeric in. Heat 1 inch of veggie or peanut oil in a medium skillet for frying. The flowers will take only a few seconds to puff up! Get them out of there and drain on a paper towel.

Sidenote
I give a choice of chili. Which you choose depends on how spicy you like it. This goes for the seeds too. Deseed if you don't want it too crazy. You can always add the seeds back in.

Coconut Rice with Herbs and Cashews

Serves 4

2 cups white rice, short-grain
One 14-ounce can coconut milk
1½ cups water, more if needed
1 teaspoon granulated sugar
  (or to taste)
Salt
1 tablespoon lime zest
1 cup chopped, toasted cashews
1 cup diced scallions, Thai basil,
  mint, cilantro, whatever you have

Regular rice is tasty and all, but it totally doesn't take advantage of being infused with flavor during the cook time. Why not swap out water for veggie stock? Or white wine? Perhaps give them a Barbie makeover and cook your grains in beet juice. The possibilities are (somewhat) endless. But of all the ways to cook rice, coconut milk is probably my favorite.

It's fragrant and rides just on the edge of sweetness, but we add tons of herbs to keep it just this side of savory. Pair it with a spicy dish like the eggplant in the next recipe and you've got the yin and yang of sweet and heat with every bite.

Clean the heck out of your rice, always. I'm talking rinse and repeat like you just dyed your hair. Once the water runs clean, place the rice, coconut milk, water, sugar, and a healthy dash of salt into a medium pot over medium heat. Once it comes to a boil, cover with a lid and simmer over medium–low heat for 15 to 20 minutes till all the liquid is absorbed and the rice is tender. If it's still al dente but the liquid is gone, just add a ½ cup or so of water. You can eat overcooked rice but not undercooked.

Let cool and fluff with a fork, adding the lime zest, half the cashews, and half the scallions. Use the rest to garnish when plated.

Garden Gimlet

Makes 1 cocktail

2 to 3 basil leaves (Thai or regular),
more for garnish
2 sliced fresh jalapeños (optional),
more for garnish
2 ounces gin (honestly, it would
be good with any clear liquor)
1 ounce lime juice
¾ ounce simple syrup

Pho is my absolute favorite soup. I remember the first time I had it. I had come out to LA to visit my friend Melissa. (You might remember her. She was the girl who thought I was eating bone marrow—see the recipe for "That Butternut Be Bone Marrow" Onion Dip on page 24.) Anyway, after several drinks and a live showing of *Pee-wee's Playhouse* (RIP Paul Reubens) we got into our first-ever fight. I'm talking 10 years of friendship, and here we were yelling on a corner in downtown LA.

The next morning, I woke up feeling like shit, emotionally and physically. But before I could try and replay the night's events in my head, Melissa walked in through the front door, both arms filled with take-out pho and fresh coconuts to soothe our morning. I don't even think we apologized to each other or remembered what the fight was even about. The broth spoke for us. I loved my friend and I really loved these new flavors I had never before tried. One of the best parts was all the accessories that it came with.

It felt a little like Build-A-Broth (trademark pending). The sides of herbs and sprouts and lime and jalapeño. It was all too much and there were so many leftovers. So after a day of digesting and watching movies in bed, I got up and had an idea. I took the limes, jalapeño, and leftover basil and designed a cocktail. A truce 'tini, if you will. But whether you are making up with a friend or just have some extra pho topping, this drink is pho'nomenal.[*]

Drop your basil and jalapeños in a shaker and muddle the heck out of them. You can leave the pepper out if you don't want spice, add an extra, or one with lots of seeds if you love.

Once that's good and worked, add the gin, lime juice, simple syrup, and ice. Shake shake shake it! Pour into a coupe or over ice and garnish with more basil and jalapeño.

[*] I'm legally obligated to make a pho pun. I don't make the rules.

Pineapple and Black Pepper Mule

Makes 1 cocktail

For the Cocktail
**1 ounce Ginger Simple Syrup
(page 229)
2 ounces vodka
1½ ounces pineapple juice
½ ounce lime juice
Seltzer to top
Crack of freshly ground pepper
Garnish of your choice**

Several things make this mule superior to the standard three-ingredient one you get served in a copper cup at your local sports bar. First, we aren't using a sickly sweet ginger beer. Instead, we're going with homemade ginger syrup. Second, pineapple juice pairs perfectly with this combo. Third, the freshly cracked pepper on top plays with the earthy heat of the ginger. But that's not all . . . .

As a millennial female who saw the 1999 Claire Danes movie *Brokedown Palace*, I have always feared that I would accidentally be caught sneaking heroin across an international border and spend the rest of my eternity in a Thai prison. Seriously. The one time I've been to Thailand, the hardest drug I had in my bag was ZzzQuil, but that didn't stop me from memorizing my lawyer's number by heart. This is a rational fear of women my age. That movie made us clinch a little tighter every time we go through customs.

In honor of this, we are keeping this drink heroin-free (shocker). But if you still want to make it a DRUG mule . . . garnish it with a little baggie with an edible in it. Turn this party up!

To a shaker of ice, add the Ginger Simple Syrup, vodka, pineapple juice, and lime juice. Shake and pour into a serving glass with ice. Top with the seltzer, then the crack of pepper. Garnish how you like and watch *Brokedown Palace* on your streaming service.

Corn and Scallion Rangoons

Serves 4

1½ cups cream cheese
½ cup cooked corn
¼ cup diced green onion
1½ teaspoons garlic powder
Salt
Pepper
8 wonton wrappers
1 egg, beaten
Peanut or vegetable oil

I know, I know. Rangoons are more of an American Midwest dish than they are Asian cuisine, but, regardless of origin, they are universally beloved because they are tasty little treats. We are skipping the crab here, no surprise, and instead going for a combo of corn and green onion for texture. If you don't love that combo, switch it up. Try diced water chestnuts and bamboo. Hell, you can make this your dessert and sub in strawberries and diced lychees and give it a sprinkle of powdered sugar.

The fact is, anything rolled around in cream cheese, stuffed in a wonton wrapper, and deep-fried is probably going to taste delicious. Serve with sweet chili sauce, soy sauce with sriracha, or whatever you prefer!

Mix the cream cheese with the corn, green onion, and garlic powder in a bowl. Add a few good cracks of salt and pepper.

Lay out your 8 wrappers, then spoon a small dollop of the mixture in the center of each. I do it all at once to make sure they're even.

Either brush or use your fingertips to trace the edges of each wonton with the egg mixture. This will be our glue to hold it together. Then, one by one, take an opposite side of the rangoon and fold together, pinching to stick. Then the other side. This is the takeout style. But any shape works if it's sealed up.

If you are frying them in oil, use peanut or veggie and get a good inch heated up to 350°F. For these, I do it in a small saucepot so it's more a deep-fried vibe. If you don't have a thermometer, drop in an extra wonton wrapper and see how it browns up. When it's good, drop them in 4 at a time until they are crispy. For an air fryer, coat the wontons in the oil (this is when spray oil comes in handy) and air fry for 10 minutes at 350°F.

Shaved Snap Pea Salad with Peanut Sauce

Serves 4

For the Salad

1 pound snap peas
1 Pickled Fresno Chili (page 228), or bird's eye chili, if you really like it hot
1 tablespoon sesame seeds
Peanut Sauce (page 229) for serving

For the Dressing

2 tablespoons olive oil
1 garlic clove, minced
1½ teaspoons lemongrass, minced
½ teaspoon red pepper flakes
Juice of two limes (about 4 tablespoons)
3 tablespoons brown sugar
2 tablespoons soy sauce

I know that it's tedious to shave enough snap peas to make a big salad. But some things are worth it, and this is one of them. Besides bathing in a bright lemongrass dressing, the shaved peas are floating on a glorious pool of what is possibly my favorite sauce of all time . . . peanut sauce.

I love peanut sauce. I would eat a dish sponge if it was dunked in peanut sauce. But I don't recommend that. Try it with this salad instead.

First, let's get to work on the snap peas! I cut them at the thinnest setting on a bias, on a mandoline, or prepare to do some knife work. Place in a bowl.

For the dressing, in a small skillet, heat the olive oil over low heat. Once it's warm, add the garlic and lemongrass. If you are using fresh lemongrass, be sure to peel back the outer layers so you are getting the tender white interior. However, nowadays, you can find a tube of minced lemongrass in the produce section, which works just as well and lasts a long time. Once that's sweated for a minute, add your red pepper flakes and stir for 30 seconds before turning off the heat and adding the lime juice, brown sugar, and soy sauce. The pan should be hot enough to dissolve the brown sugar.

You can either cool the warm vinaigrette or pour it warm over your shaved snap peas. Toss all around to incorporate. Plate with a nice pool of Peanut Sauce (page 229) on the bottom with the snap peas piled high on top. Garnish with the sesame seeds and Pickled Fresno Chilies (page 228).

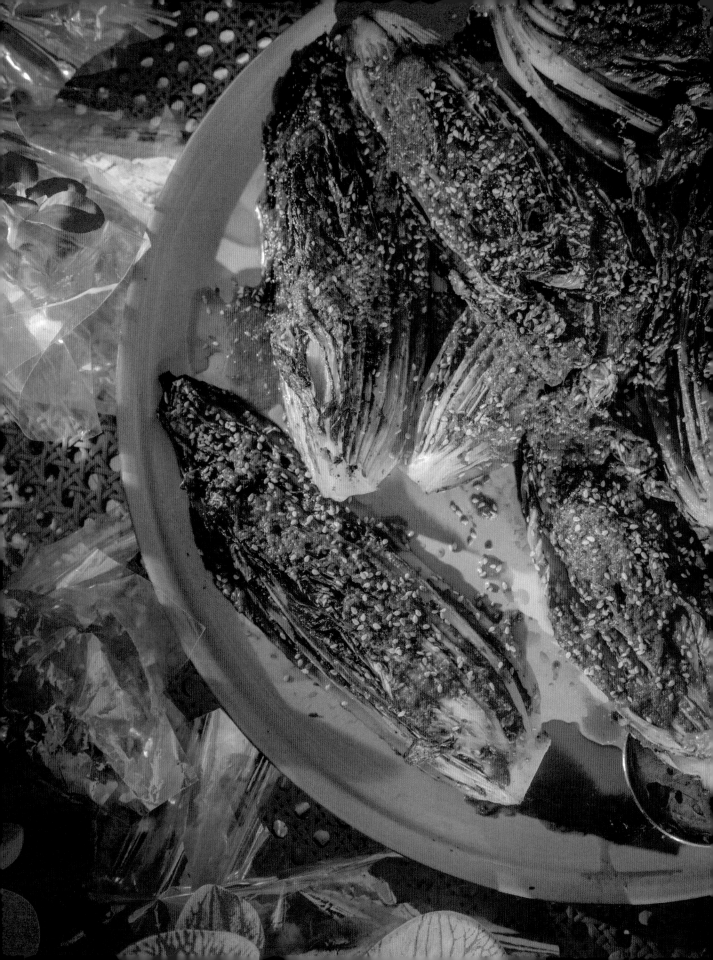

Charred Cabbage with Red Curry Butter

Serves 4

4 tablespoons (½ stick) unsalted
  butter, room temperature
1 heaping tablespoon red
  curry paste
One big head Napa or
  Savoy cabbage
2 tablespoons vegetable oil
Sesame seeds, toasted peanuts,
  or fresh herbs for garnish

I remember the first time I saw a cabbage cut into hearty wedges and given a good sear. It was in a cooking magazine, and I was oddly proud of what I saw. I know that sounds ridiculous, but I have a tendency to anthropomorphize things, and a brassica is no different.

What I mean by proud is that, finally, people were seeing that cabbage wasn't just filler in an eggroll. Or the least popular ingredient in a stir-fry. Sure, it doesn't have the boldest of flavors, but that's why it works so well in something like . . . this dish. Consider cabbage to be the base that holds up the pungent curry-packed butter. Cabbage is the canvas. But, without a canvas, you can't have the art. Holy smokes, that sounded smart.

In a small bowl, whip together the butter and curry paste. Cut the cabbage either into quarters or sixths, depending on the size of the cabbage, lengthwise through the core. Heat the oil over medium–high heat in a large cast-iron skillet. You want it hot but not smoking. Lay down the cabbage, cut side down, and let it sear for 2 minutes before flipping to the other side.

Once both sides have some char to them, flip them on their backs, add the butter to the pan, and turn heat to medium–low. Allow the butter to melt, then baste these bad boys by tilting the pan. All the butter will puddle at the bottom, so use a spoon to spoon the melted butter over the cabbage.

Plate the cabbage and pour any remaining butter over the top. Sprinkle with some garnish.

Sidenote

This dish is also delicious using bok choy, but most things are delicious when coated in a bold butter.

Go Go Gochujang Eggplant Ribs

Serves 4

For the Ribs
2 pounds Chinese or Japanese eggplant (about 5 skinny eggplants)
Salt

For the Go Go Sauce
¼ cup gochujang
¼ cup tomato paste
½ cup water
2 tablespoons sesame oil
2 tablespoons honey
¼ cup rice vinegar
1 garlic clove, finely grated or minced

For the Garnishes
Sesame seeds
Chopped scallions and cilantro

No other vegetable has benefited quite as much by the world of emojis as the eggplant. Who would've guessed! But despite its PR glow-up, there are still a lot of people who don't get down with this nightshade. This dish might change that.

What's with the "go go"? Well, that's because we are using gochujang in our sauce. If you've never had it, welcome to your new life. Gochujang is a fermented bean paste that brings umami to everything it touches. It's a staple in Korean cooking, and I find it pairs perfectly with tender Japanese or Chinese eggplant. Even Fairy Tale eggplant. The more compact the better. Sometimes big ol' slices of regular globe eggplants can be intimidating to an eggplant-apprehensive person.

Slap these slightly spicy, sticky ribs on top of a bed of cooling Coconut Rice (page 193) for the perfect combo.

Preheat the oven to 400°F. Cut the eggplants in half lengthwise, then make crisscross score marks with a knife on the cut side. Set the eggplant on a paper towel and sprinkle the scored side with salt. Let it be for 10 minutes as the salt pulls out excess moisture. You will see water beading up on the eggplant like it just finished a Zumba class. Wipe them down to take off this extra moisture and added salt, which will help keep your eggplant from getting all chewy.

For the go go sauce: In a small pot, whisk together all the go go ingredients over low to medium heat, just until they all come together.

To a medium baking dish, add a little of the sauce to the bottom before laying the eggplant, score side down, into it. Pour half the sauce over the eggplant, making sure all the exposed tops are coated. Place in the oven for 15 minutes before flipping the eggplants up, brushing with the remaining marinade, then sticking them back in the oven for another 10 minutes. Once the eggplants feel tender, I like to hit them with a 2- to 3-minute broil on high just to char the edges and give them little burnt ends. Scatter sesame seeds, chopped scallions, and cilantro over the top.

Spiked Cardamom Coffee

Makes 1 cocktail

For the Cardamom Coffee
½ tablespoon cardamom for every
    cup of grounds you brew

For the Cocktail
6 ounces (standard cup size) of
    cardamom coffee
2 ounces dark rum
1 ounce condensed milk,
    more if desired
½ teaspoon almond (traditional)
    or vanilla extract
½ teaspoon cardamom
Splash of Kahlua, Baileys,
    chocolate liqueur, or others
    (optional), more if desired

This coffee cocktail would be great the morning after a blow-out dinner party. But sometimes you need it beforehand when you really want to Thai one on . . . .

And if you didn't need one before that pun, I bet you do now. Thai iced coffee is delicious and creamy and almost feels like a dessert, which is totally OK to have in the morning. After all, people will eat an 8,000-calorie stack of rocky road pancakes to start their day and we all pretend that's normal!

You can follow the recipe, or you can deviate from it if you feel like adding in different liqueurs or spices. Hint: Make it without alcohol if you have work to do and just want a tasty caffeine jolt.

To make your cardamom coffee, simply add the ground cardamom (or grind your own cardamom pods) to the coffee grinds before you brew. Next, prepare your nose because if you thought the smell of regular coffee was enough to get you out of bed, cardamom wafting through the air will have you floating nose-first to your kitchen.

Mix the cocktail ingredients in the glass before adding ice. If you are making a batch at once, up your quantities and mix everything together in a pitcher without ice and let folks pour it themselves.

You can top it with a little more condensed milk or Kahlua for the pretty swirl effect. Now take a big swig for the energy push you need to get started on your savory Crispy Rice Waffle (page 209) to balance out the sweet.

Morning-After Fill: Crispy Rice Waffle

Makes 1 waffle

Leftovers

1 cup Coconut Rice with Herbs and Cashews (page 193)
½ cup chopped Charred Cabbage with Red Curry Butter (page 203), Go Go Gochujang Eggplant Ribs (page 205), or snap peas from Shaved Snap Pea Salad with Peanut Sauce (page 229)
Roasted Mango Salsa (page 192) or Peanut Sauce (page 229) for garnish

New Ingredients

1 egg
1 tablespoon soy sauce
Cooking spray

Fried rice is a go-to leftover meal that comes in clutch. But sometimes I want MORE. I want to do my leftover rice justice. And that's when it's time to bust out the waffle iron. As I've stated before, I'm a massive fan of Waffle House and this gives me an opportunity to get my role-play on. If I'm feeling really frisky, I'll put on a name tag. Consider topping the waffle with a fried egg.

This one couldn't be easier.

Decide which leftovers you want in your waffle and dice them up well. The eggplant is delicious. The snap peas are great. Cabbage is exquisite. The general ratio that I like is for every cup of rice used, add ½ cup chopped veggies, 1 egg, and 1 tablespoon of soy sauce. It works better if you reheat the rice and veggies before adding the egg and soy. Once you've got your mixture heated and mixed . . .

Throw a big glop of it in the hot, oiled waffle iron and use it like you would a normal waffle. Remove it when it's nice and crispy and the egg has cooked through from the heat.

Drizzle with the Peanut Sauce (page 229) or dip in Roasted Mango Salsa (page 192). Whichever you like. This is one of those meals where the leftovers might even be better than the night before.

MEAL FOR A GODDESS

Treat your guests like royalty
and treat your stomach royally.

This meal might seem out of left field, but sometimes you and your friends need to throw on some gold kaftans, buy a $10 thing of edible gold leaf, and make yourselves feel like the queens that you are. Be extra!

Let it be known, this meal is not gender specific. But it is specifically opulent, filled with all the things that make me feel decadent. Luxurious. We end the meal by hand-feeding our guests boozy grapes . . . need I say more?

RECIPES

Raspberry and Rose Spritz

Makes 1 cocktail

This drink could not be more fit for a goddess, as it features both champagne and roses! Specifically, rose water. A controversial ingredient, no doubt. One too many drops and you are drinking potpourri. Luckily, I have a solution for that.

I like to keep my rose water in an atomizer and only spray the finished drink with it rather than add any to the drink itself. Plus, you get to shop for cute empty bottles, and then act like you're Elizabeth Taylor in a perfume ad from the '80s as you walk around your guests with it, spraying the top of their bubbles.

5 raspberries
1 ounce gin
½ ounce lemon juice
¼ ounce simple syrup
Brut champagne or prosecco
Rose water in an atomizer

In an empty shaker, toss in 4 of the raspberries and 5 raspberries and muddle till you can't muddle any more. Add the lemon juice, simple syrup, and ice. Shake it up, then pour through a fine mesh strainer into a flute to catch any seeds. You need to have patience during this. Just when you think you got them all out, there's probably a little more hiding in there. The drink will be a gorgeous vibrant pink color.

Fill the rest of your flute with champagne, plop in that last raspberry, then spray 2 spritzes of rose water on the top.

Beluga Lentil Caviar

Serves 4

Caviar is one of those things that looks like a fun thing to eat. A little build-your-own pile of decadence. Feel free to use the real stuff if you married rich and love it, but in this case . . . we are using lentils! Serve them with all the usual caviar suspects: crème fraîche, dill, minced shallots, etc. But I don't want us getting too cocky, so we are serving them on Pringles.

1 cup dried black beluga lentils
1 tablespoon olive oil
2 garlic cloves, minced
3 cups water
1 tablespoon vegan dashi powder
1 tablespoon capers, chopped
2 tablespoons soy sauce
1 tablespoon caper brine
A few dashes of your favorite hot sauce,
  I prefer Cholula with this
Salt
Pepper
Pringles for serving

Rinse the lentils thoroughly. In a medium pot, add a tablespoon or so of olive oil and sauté the garlic for 1 to 2 minutes. Add the water to the pot and bring to a boil. If you're going for full ocean flavor, add your dashi here. Once the water is bubbling, add the lentils and turn down the heat to a simmer. Cover for 15 to 20 minutes.

Once the lentils are tender but holding their shape, drain any remaining water and mix in the capers, soy sauce, brine, and hot sauce. Salt and pepper to taste.

Serve in your fanciest dish with your finest Pringles and start talking in a pompous accent.

Walnut Merguez Peppadews

Serves 4

For the Merguez

2 cups walnuts
½ teaspoon cumin seeds
½ teaspoon coriander seeds
½ teaspoon fennel seeds
1 tablespoon olive oil
½ onion, diced
2 garlic cloves, chopped
1 teaspoon paprika
2 tablespoon tomato paste
1 tablespoon harissa
½ cup fresh cilantro

For Serving

A dozen or more peppadew
  peppers (red and yellow)
1 cup crumbled feta

The first time I ever even heard of merguez sausage, I was working in a café in NYC during Pride weekend. We had flatbread as a special with this spicy African sausage on it. An hour into brunch, it sold out, but the ordering system said we still had them. So, I'm there at the counter, punching in orders for a table of six very in-shape, gorgeous men, when my stressed expeditor runs out of the kitchen screaming, "No merguez! No merguez!"

But with this Iranian accent, it sounded like "no more gays." You could hear a feather drop. And one probably did, because there were a lot of boas that morning.

Needless to say, I immediately ran to my section to explain that it wasn't what it sounded like. Honestly, they were less upset about the possible slur and more upset they couldn't get the flatbread.

This is my take on a merguez appetizer, except we are using the mighty walnut as our "meat" and an antipasti bar staple—peppadews—that I don't think get enough play! They look like tiny rubies.

For the merguez, first soak the walnuts. Place them in a medium heat-safe bowl or pot, ideally with a lid. Boil water in a kettle and pour the scalding water over the walnuts. Cover and let soak for at least an hour and up to overnight. Reserve ½ cup of the soaking water.

Preheat the oven to 400°F. In a dry, small pan over low heat, toast the cumin seeds, coriander seeds, and fennel seeds for 1 to 2 minutes till fragrant. Set to the side. Using the same pan, heat the olive oil before adding the onions and garlic. Stir for 3 to 4 minutes until they are translucent.

To a food processor, add the onions and garlic, soaked walnuts, toasted seeds, paprika, tomato paste, harissa, cilantro, and the reserved soaking water. Pulse the mixture till it has a chunky, ground meat texture.

If your peppadews are jarred in oil, be sure to give them a rinse under water and pat them dry with a paper towel, making sure you get any water hiding in the hollow inside. Then, one by one, stuff the peppadews with the walnut mixture (I use a tiny espresso spoon or my hands), then top each pepper with a chunk of feta, sealing in the merguez. Pack it down before placing on a pan, feta side up. Bake 10 minutes.

Extra Tip

Serve with Tahini Sauce (page 229) or a creamy labneh blended with whatever herbs you can get your hands on—cilantro, parsley, scallions—to make a quick dipping sauce.

Mini Golden Tahdigs

Serves 4

For the Tahdigs

¼ cup plain yogurt
2 tablespoons turmeric
2 tablespoons minced garlic
1 egg
Salt
Pepper
4 cups cooked basmati rice or
   saffron rice
Neutral cooking oil

Optional Garnish

Dried currants or cherries
Parsley
Toasted pumpkin seeds

Aka crispy Persian rice. Anything you can crack into like a crème brûlée is my food weakness. This rice is toothsome. Exciting. It makes other rice look bland. However, it can also be dangerous. Everybody wants the crusty edges and, you better believe, I will fight for it. Rather than have one of your guests get stabbed with a fork trying to get to the good bits, we are making eight individual tahdigs. Crust for everyone!

Sidenote

I'm starting this recipe with cooked basmati rice. Whether you buy it precooked or make it yourself, I am just trusting you to get to this part of the journey on your own.

Preheat the oven to 450°F.

In a large bowl, mix the yogurt, turmeric, garlic, egg, and a good amount of salt and pepper. The yogurt should be a gorgeous gold color. Then fold in the rice.

Oil a muffin tin, then fill it with the rice mixture (should make 8) before putting it in a 450°F oven for 15 minutes. Cover with foil, then go for another 15. What you're left with is personal-sized tahdigs. Sprinkle them with your garnishes and pocket a few tahdigs while no one is looking.

What a Nice Pear

Makes 1 cocktail

For the Pear Puree
MAKES ENOUGH FOR 8 DRINKS
1 or 2 pears (I like Barlett)
1 tablespoon cloves
1 cinnamon stick
1 tablespoon lemon juice
1 tablespoon sugar

For the Cocktail
1 tablespoon fresh rosemary needles, plus a sprig for garnish
1 ounce pear puree
2 ounces bourbon
1½ ounces lemon juice
Club soda or ginger beer (optional)

Out of context, the name of this drink sounds like something you would hear catcalled when walking past a construction site. Maybe a construction site from the 1920s. It's innocent enough, unlike this drink, with its punch of bourbon, rosemary, cloves, and cinnamon.

And like most of the fruit purees for cocktails in this book, this one is also great when simply added to champagne. It's got all those cozy fall flavors and is a perfect thing to tipple on Turkey Day morning before the family starts fighting.

Preheat the oven to 350°F. Give your pears a rough chop, being sure to remove the core and seeds. Place the pears, cloves, and cinnamon in a square of foil, then toss in the lemon juice and sugar. Wrap tightly in a teardrop shape, completely closed, then place on a sheet pan in case of spillage. Stick in the oven for 30 minutes or until the pears are totally soft. Remove from the oven and discard the cloves and cinnamon stick. Blend the cooked pears till smooth. Don't be discouraged that it is not the prettiest puree. It will taste delicious. If you have some left over, store in an airtight container in the fridge and spread that goodness on a buttered biscuit like jam later in the week!

In an empty shaker, muddle the rosemary to release the fragrant oils. Then add the 1 ounce of puree, bourbon, lemon juice, and ice and shake it all up. Strain over ice to get the rosemary needles out and garnish with the rosemary sprig. If you prefer a little more effervescence, top with club soda or ginger beer.

Roasted Beets with Blue Cheese and Balsamic

Serves 4

**6 medium raw beets (I like a mix
   of red and golden)**
2 tablespoons olive oil
1 tablespoon honey
**1 cup sweet white onion,
   thinly sliced**
Store-bought balsamic glaze
Pomegranate seeds for garnish
**10 ounces crumbled blue or goat
   cheese for garnish**
Sprigs of dill for garnish

A cool thing about this recipe is you can absolutely make it ahead of time. The beets themselves take an hour, so you can knock that out the day before and have them chilling in the fridge. Make a few extra if you are thinking of making the Morning-After Fill (page 226). Even if you don't, they are great to chop up for salads the rest of the week. And did I mention they are gorgeous?! For being a root veggie that lots of people complain tastes like dirt, they sure look like expensive gems sitting on a platter.

Your guests won't know whether to eat this dish or be scared that a security detail from Harry Winston is about to tackle them.

Preheat the oven to 400°F.

Whenever I peel raw beets, it looks like there was a murder in my kitchen. So, instead, I wait until after the beets are cooked to peel them. It is so much easier. First, clean the heck out of the beets and trim any stem. Take a fork and poke some holes in each beet, which will allow them to steam.

Now, let's wrap these beets. I take a foot of foil and simply wrap each beet individually like an old-school baked potato. Because beet juice will leak out, double-check to make sure they are wrapped well and stick them on a pan before popping in the oven for an hour.

Once the beets are tender, let them cool. To peel, run them under water while using your hands to gently peel off the skin like you would to peel a hard-boiled egg. Slice the peeled beets and toss them in the olive oil and honey.

Arrange the beet slices and onion as if you are creating a masterpiece, dotting with the balsamic glaze. Garnish with a sprinkling of pomegranate seeds, crumbled cheese, and little sprigs of dill. Make a pun such as "Drop a beet!" or just start beatboxing until your guests groan loudly.

MEAL FOR A GODDESS

Brown Butter "Scallops" with Tarragon and Capers

Serves 4

Two 14-ounce cans or jars of
  hearts of palm
1 tablespoon Old Bay Seasoning
3 tablespoons unsalted butter
½ cup capers
Juice of half a lemon
1 tablespoon fresh tarragon leaves

Ever since Venus popped out of that giant scallop shell, courtesy of Botticelli, scallops have been associated with feminine energy. Goddesses. And, let's be honest, the shells give vulva vibes. But for most people, scallops just mean you're about to have something delicious in your mouth. Why should vegetarians miss out? Enter, heart of palm.

Heart of palm is the master of pretending to be seafood. The Meryl Streep of shellfish. She can play crab. Squid. Or today's role: scallops. It's a star turn with the saltiness of capers, the nutty sweetness of the brown butter, and the licorice tinge of tarragon.

Try to pick out the thickest hearts that give you a good scallop size. Ideally 1 inch in diameter. You can usually get a good 4 or 5 hearts per can or jar but sometimes they have fallen apart, which is why I suggest buying two cans. You can usually get 3 or 4 "scallops" out of a palm. Then cut them into scallop shapes, pat them dry with a paper towel, and give them a sprinkle of Old Bay Seasoning on either side.

Heat a large skillet over medium or medium–high heat and add 1 tablespoon of the butter. Once melted, add in the palm scallops! Hear that sizzle. Flip after 2 minutes, or until you get that sear. After the other side has seared, take the scallops out of the pan and put them to the side.

Add the remaining butter to the pan to brown with the capers. Turn down the heat to medium–low and keep a close eye on this. Once you see the edges start to turn a little brown, start swirling. Keep doing this for 3 to 4 minutes, until the butter gets a golden-brown color and it starts to smell nutty. Congrats, you've made brown butter!

Add the lemon juice and tarragon and turn down the heat to low. Cook for a minute before adding the hearts of palm back in. Baste the "scallops" with the sauce for a minute or so to warm the scallops back up before plating.

Elderflower and Champagne Frozen Grapes

Serves 4 to 6

**2 pounds grapes (individual
   grapes or broken into
   smaller clusters)
2 cups vodka
½ cup St-Germain
Bottle of cheap prosecco**

What? A cocktail you can chew? WILD. Look, I first saw frozen champagne grapes when I was perusing Pinterest for cute girls'-night-in ideas. But they were always off the vine and covered in sugar. No, thank you. I want to be fed them like I'm a Grecian god. And I want them to pack a punch. You're going to want to pull these out and serve immediately, because the booze will thaw them out fast. You could even serve them in mini clusters.

One tip that has helped me get more booze into the grapes is to take a toothpick and prick a couple of holes in each of them. You don't need to do this if you are taking the grapes off the stem, as there will be an exposed spot where the stem was. But if you go whole cluster, prick those things.

Take a container big enough to hold the cluster. Before you put them in the container, add the vodka and St-Germain to it. Lay the grapes on top, then add the prosecco until the grapes are covered. Marinate overnight.

The next day, drain out the grapes and freeze for at least 4 hours. Take out and serve immediately, ideally straight into your guests' mouths while they lay on the floor.

Extra Tip
I put a little St-Germain in a spray bottle and give the grapes a misting halfway through freezing.

Let yourself be Dionysus for the day.

Morning-After Fill: Moroccan Chili Fries

Serves 2

Leftovers

1 cup Beluga Lentil Caviar (page 213) or 1 cup of your favorite beans
6 or so Walnut Merguez Peppadews (page 214)
OR
1 cup Walnut Merguez by itself (page 214), plus more merguez if available
A few red beet slices from Roasted Beets with Blue Cheese and Balsamic (page 221)

Extra Ingredients

1 bag of frozen fries (I like a 28-ounce bag of waffle cut)
1 tablespoon olive oil
1 tablespoon cumin
1 teaspoon ground cinnamon
One 28-ounce can of crushed tomatoes
1 tablespoon harissa (optional)
Cheese (optional)
1 cup sour cream or yogurt
Scallion or cilantro (optional)
Pickled Onions (optional; page 228)

If french fries were a human, they'd be an EMT. They can save a life, ya'll. Even more so when they are piled high with a delicious, protein-packed spicy chili. But not just any chili, a Moroccan-spiced chili. You'll get the earthiness of cumin mixed with that little warming heat of cinnamon.

If you want to make fries from scratch, I get it. This chili would also be delicious over a baked potato or leftover crispy rice, on the small chance any remains. Even just a heaping bowl by itself with Pringles for dipping will fix you right up.

Get fries cooking in the oven or air fryer (follow the package instructions). I went with waffle fries but regular fries, tater tots, or even sweet potato fries work great too. While that's happening . . .

Give your Beluga Lentil Caviar a rinse to get off some of the soy sauce and caper brine. If you don't have the lentils, you can always add a can of beans.

In a Dutch oven or large pot, heat the olive oil before adding the cumin and cinnamon. Give a quick stir to let the oil release before adding in the chopped leftovers. Stir for a minute, then add the tomatoes, lentils, any chopped peppadews, and leftover extra merguez, until it's a good chili ratio of tomato to veg. Simmer for 8 to 10 minutes and let all the flavors marry. If you want it a little spicier, add a tablespoonful of harissa.

Pile that chili high on top of your fries. If you want cheese, pile it on, then hit it under the broiler to melt. Stick the beets in a blender with sour cream for a pink pop to drizzle on top. Garnish with herbs and pickled onions to really set it off.

Appendix:
Sauces, Syrups, and Garnishes

Pickled Onions

1 small red onion, sliced thin
½ cup apple cider vinegar
1 tablespoon sugar
1 tablespoon salt

Pack the onions into a glass, sealable jar. Heat all the other ingredients in a small pot until boiling, ensuring the sugar and salt have dissolved, then take off the heat. Let it cool for a few minutes until it's just warm.

Pour the warm pickling liquid into the jar of onions. Wait till it's cooled to put on the lid. They will keep in the fridge for up to 2 weeks!

Pickled Fresno Chilies

See the previous recipe. Just use thinly sliced Fresno chilies instead of red onions.

Coconut Bacon

2 cups unsweetened coconut flakes
2½ tablespoons tamari (if using soy, just do 2 tablespoons)
2 tablespoons olive oil
1½ tablespoons maple syrup
1 teaspoon liquid smoke
1 teaspoon smoked paprika

Preheat the oven to 350°F. Place all the ingredients in a medium bowl. Massage the coconut flakes in the mixture and let marinate for 20 minutes.

After marinating, spread the flakes on a parchment-lined baking sheet. Cook for 10 to 12 minutes, stirring halfway through, but keep an eye on it. One minute too long and that maple syrup can burn. You want it crisped up with that "bacon" smell wafting out.

Pistachio Pesto

3 cups basil leaves
1 cup roasted pistachios
½ cup grated Parmesan
2 garlic cloves, more if needed
Pinch of red pepper flakes
1 cup olive oil, more if needed
1 lemon, zested then juiced, more if needed

Combine the basil, pistachios, Parmesan, garlic, red pepper flakes, and olive oil in a food processor. Add the lemon juice and half the zest. Blend until you've got a perfect pesto consistency. If it's too dry, add more olive oil. If it tastes flat, add more garlic and lemon juice. Pesto is personal.

Hazelnut Salsa Macha

4 garlic cloves
1 medium shallot
½ cup hazelnuts (but could use whichever nut you prefer)
3 to 4 dried guajillo chilies
1 cup olive oil
1 teaspoon coriander seeds (if you don't have them, can use ground)
2 tablespoons apple cider or white vinegar
1 tablespoon sesame seeds
1 tablespoon pepitas (optional)

First, give your garlic, shallot, and hazelnuts a rough chop. We want a little more surface area for toasting, but it'll eventually go in a food processor so don't be too precious about it. Next, remove the stems from the chilies. Break them up a little and discard all the seeds. I break out the pandemic stash of plastic gloves for this!

In a medium sauté pan, heat the olive oil over medium before adding the garlic, hazelnuts, and coriander. If you are using ground coriander, wait to add in the next step. You want to sweat the garlic and lightly toast the nuts and coriander seeds before adding the chilies. Stir 2 to 3 minutes, then take off the heat and cool.

Dump all this goodness in a food processor along with the vinegar and sesame seeds. I prefer keeping my sesame seeds raw, but if you want them toasted, go for it. Give it some good blending pulses to get it all to combine with still a little texture. You want a salsa, not a sauce. I like to add in some toasted whole pepitas at the end for extra texture. This will store in an airtight container for up to a month, but I doubt it'll be there that long. Put it on breakfast tacos! Add a dollop to a creamy soup! Use it to make spicy bread crumbs!

Tahini Sauce

½ **cup tahini**
3 to 4 tablespoons water, more if needed
3 tablespoons lemon juice, more if needed
2 garlic cloves
1 tablespoon olive oil, more if needed
Salt
Pepper

Put everything in a blender or food processor. Or if you aren't using one, just make sure to mince the heck out of the garlic before whisking everything together. If it's too thin, add more water or oil. Too bland? Perhaps more lemon or a little garlic. Taste and assess; you've got this!

Ginger Simple Syrup

1 cup sugar
1 cup water
2-inch knob of ginger, peeled and roughly chopped

In a small saucepan over medium–low heat, combine the sugar, water, and ginger. Heat up and whisk till the sugar is dissolved, then turn the heat to low to continue cooking 4 to 5 minutes. You do not want the syrup to reduce but just to give it time for the ginger to infuse. Take the pan off the heat and strain out the chunks of ginger.

Peanut Sauce

1 cup creamy peanut butter
2 tablespoons soy sauce
2 tablespoons rice wine vinegar
1 tablespoon ginger, more if needed
1 tablespoon honey or maple syrup, more if needed
Juice of half a lime, more if needed
1 garlic clove
Pinch of red pepper flakes

The first thing you need to do is scoop out a spoonful of peanut butter and eat it. That's an order.

Combine the ingredients in a food processor and blend until smooth. That's it! Then taste to your liking. Too acidic? Add more honey. Too sweet? Throw in some more ginger or lime juice. And if it feels too thick, a splash of water can work without diluting the taste.

Acknowledgments

First, I'd like to acknowledge anyone who has actually bought this book and, therefore, is able to read this first line in the acknowledgments. You're the best!

This book would not exist without Claire Thomas. She did everything from the photography to letting us cook the food in her kitchen and to turning her garage into a photo studio. She is the other half of my dolphin brain. Claire, I love you! Now, everyone, go buy her Sweet Laurel Bakery books after this.

It also wouldn't have come together without my crew: Yayo Ahumada, Leo Levy, Shellie Anderson, Emily Pertzborn, Mia Radcliffe, Melissa McSorley, Garret Logan, and Adam Smith.

To my editor, Ann Treistman, and everyone at Countryman Press! This was my first cookbook, which required some handholding. So thank you for doing just that and also fielding 9,000 emails. To Evi.O-Studio, for the beautiful design, and Allison Chi, for all her guidance.

Thanks to Abigail Walters, who believed in this thing even when it was a sloppy proposal. A dream agent! The same for Vincent Nastri, who supports me and all my endeavors and has for over a decade.

Thank you to my guy, Chip, for being a constant source of encouragement through this whole process and my #1 taste tester. You are my favorite person to share a meal and a cocktail with.

All my friends have taken turns being a support system when I needed them, but special shout-out to Grace, Jaclyn, Kiwi, Melissa, and Ashleigh, who hid their eye rolls when I would not stop stressing. Bless y'all.

I'd also like to thank my dear friend, Matthew Mills, who gave me my first job ever writing about food and let me do sketch comedy on the actual *Iron Chef* set. A career highlight, tbh.

And finally . . . to my mom, Carolyn, for somehow keeping this vegetarian fed in rural North Carolina in the '90s. To my dad and stepmom, Anne, for introducing me to the glory of all things Food Network, which, quite frankly, changed the chemistry of my brain.